Selflovology

Your Journey to Self-Love Starts Here

By **Armon Anderson, Mr. Self-Love**

MORRIGHAN PUBLISHING
where your words come to life

ISBN: 978-1-7342355-9-3 (Hardback)

Library of Congress Control Number: 2021903846

First printing edition 2021. This edition published and arranged by Morrighan Publishing with special thanks to:

Melvyn Paulino
Graphic designer, Book Layout
melvynpaulino.com

Meredith Dunn
Freedom Press
Author Coaching + Consulting
FreedomPress.org

Cherie Foxley
Graphic Design & Book Cover Artist
cheriefox.com

Acknowledgements

"The more you praise and celebrate your life, the more there is in life to celebrate."

Oprah Winfrey

I have to start by thanking my mother and sister for raising and mentoring me, and loving me unconditionally as I went through my journey to discovering self-love.

Also, I'd like to thank my incredible lady for reading early drafts, giving me advice about the direction of the book, and supporting and believing in my life vision.

Lastly, I want to thank you—my friends and supporters, new and old. Thank you for always sharing my vision and reminding me why I do what I do. You inspire me and amaze me with the self-awareness you use to face what truly matters in life.

Table of Contents

Introduction

Why This Book?
Why Now? Why You?

> *"You can learn how to be you in time. It's easy. All you need is love."*
>
> **The Beatles**

We all love a good love story. It's part of our humanity to love and to seek love from others. Love is a unique human experience that we all share.

We all are born with the innate need for love. We learn the rhythms of love from our immediate care givers. If our care givers haven't learned to love themselves, heal their own personal heartbreaks, and evolve, we end up with courtside seats to witness their un-healed wounds in real time. We internalize what we see from our caregivers, and we take on their ideas of love—whether healthy or not.

Our early interactions with love color and inform everything we do in our lives. We all desire love and to give love in return, so why are we so negligent in the area of self-love...? Why do we continue deny-ing ourselves the very thing we deserve? Why aren't we taught at an early age that in order to really love someone, we must love our-selves first? After all, we cannot fill if we are not filled ourselves.

Why don't we hear more people talking about falling in love with themselves? We talk to our friends about our dates, and how much we like or love our significant other, husband, or friends. However, when's the last time you heard someone talking about falling in love with themselves?

Here's the truth: Falling in love with yourself is complicated and hard. Even more so because no one teaches us that it is an important part of a healthy and fulfilling life. We are taught to give, give, give, and we aren't taught that receiving is an essential part of healthy living.

It is especially difficult if you don't even know yourself—your true self, the person who you are deep down when no one else is looking. How can you love someone you don't take the time to know and understand? The reality is you can't love yourself fully until you get to know yourself on the deepest possible levels.

Many of us hold our hearts safe, so safe in fact, that we've created walls around it that even we can't permeate. Where did we learn that? What is that about? What was the pain that led us to armoring up, as if we are going to war with someone when the war is really within ourselves? Yes, I am sure that last question hit pretty deep. And believe it or not, that is a great starting point.

We have become robotic and have detached from our basic needs because we feel like we have to protect ourselves, when "protecting" ultimately leads to suppressing our joy, who we truly are, and slowly diminishing the love we carry for ourselves.

But here's the good news: You *can* learn to love yourself. You simply have to meet and get to know your truest self. Sound silly? I thought so too—until I went on this revolutionary journey of self-love and personal development.

Teaching people about self-love means showing them how to show up as their true selves and living out their truth each and every day. Teaching self-love means equipping, empowering, and unleashing people to step up and take control of their own lives and how they interact with others and within the world.

This self-awareness and recognition of the humanity in all people around us cultivates even more self-awareness, and has the capacity to put an end to self-loathing, bullying, violence, and negativity that's spreading like wildfire in contemporary society. Through self-awareness and self-growth, we can improve our own lives, the lives of those we love, the lives of those within our communities, and the lives of the next generation.

This is critical. It is important work that must be done. It must not be ignored.

If each of us would fully commit to this process and take ownership of it in our own lives we would begin to see a shift—not only in our own lives, but in the families and communities around us and ultimately the world. What a beautiful picture this is… Imagine it for a moment. One person's decision to love themselves without reservation is like a pebble dropped in still waters. The ripple effects are huge and unending—world-changing.

When we truly understand, accept, and love ourselves we can lead by example and live in love and light. Self-love is contagious—like a beacon of light attracting others. It refines our purpose and direction in the world. It allows us to be the best versions of ourselves each and every day. Self-love helps us to understand how and why we exist in the world. Though largely overlooked and ignored this work is vital to living a full and abundant life. It is critical to a life of joy and deep connection with the people around you. It is the most revolutionary work we can do—to learn to truly accept, understand, and love ourselves despite everything we have been taught.

First and foremost, let me tell you that the process of finding self-love isn't always as easy and glamorous as it's portrayed on social media. Please do not confuse self-love with self-care. While both are equally valuable and important, they are not the same.

Self-love is not long walks on the beach, hot baths, golf vacations, and curling up with a good book. Self-love is staring deep into your soul and truly seeing who you are at your deepest core. Self-love sees everything that you have been through and freely offers gratitude, forgiveness, and unconditional acceptance for all that has made you the person you are today.

This level of deep reflection and recognition is far from glamorous. It can, and likely will, be the hardest thing you ever set out to do. The process can be confusing, exhausting, and you may often feel like you are not making any progress. But you are! Even small shifts, like the pebble in the pond, are creating ripple effects that you may not see right away. This process takes commitment and resolve to see it through no matter how slow going it is. It all matters. And it is making a difference. You have to trust the process.

Believe me, I have been there. I have been at the beginning of the journey just like you are today. It feels scary and your mind will try to tell you that you aren't worth the work. I am here to tell you that you are worth it, and it is the most important work you will ever do!

By writing out my life experiences and my long journey to finding self-love on paper, I've learned the most beautiful thing: how to be gentle with myself and love myself for the place I am in, every step of my journey.

The stories I'm about to relay to you have all been monumentally important to my discovery of self-love. No matter where you are in your process, know that you are right where you need to be. And together, we'll get you from where you are to where you want to be.

Let's start with the night when I finally hit rock bottom. Trust me when I say that I felt like I'd hit this point many times prior to this moment, but it wasn't until I saw a girl I thought I loved hitting me as I sat motionless in a car—unable to decipher how I'd let myself get to this place—that I knew what hitting rock bottom really felt like. But first, let me back up and tell you exactly how I ended up in that car in Encino at 1 am. Then I can explain why that breaking point was the best moment of my life, to this day.

That night, I was faced with a point in my life in which I had to choose to stay the same or grow. Thankfully, I chose to grow. This book is my life's purpose. It is the gift from the pain that I endured. It is the result of painful and chilling moments. This book, with its message, is the sole reason I choose to wake up every single day to not only survive in this world, but thrive and to inspire others to do so as well. This book is a love letter to myself and the world. My testimony. My whole life. This is why I was born. I hope this is the beginning of your own self-love journey. I'm honored to be a part of your path.

Chapter 1

Choosing Betterness, Not Bitterness

> *"Bitterness is like cancer. It eats upon the host. It doesn't do anything to the object of its displeasure."*
>
> **Maya Angelou**

When I listen to other people, they frequently cite one or two memorable experiences that have colored who they think they can be, and they're usually traumatic. The hard times and problematic people in our lives leave an impression on us that can be hard to shake. Most of the time, people just keep struggling with the impact of trauma, and remain bitter about the bad things that have happened to them.

The most powerful moments in our lives often occur when we're faced with challenges, although this fact may not always be evident at the time. The saying "you live and learn" is true, especially in relation to self-mastery. The faster you recognize your difficult moments as potential catalysts for self-growth, the faster you'll learn that the actions you take after they occur will determine your life course. But first, we might need some time to consider how we can make better choices.

Trust me, this process isn't easy. In fact, it can be much more difficult to be grateful for the natural ebb and flow of life than to remain bitter, hold grudges, and feel like it's you against the world. Learning not to be bitter means becoming acutely aware of yourself, and not allowing circumstances to change who you fundamentally are at your core. The more self-love you have, the easier this shift in your mindset becomes. For me, I faced this fact when I was twelve years old...

It started out as an average Tuesday, as a typical twelve-year-old boy. I remember it like it was yesterday. As I woke up in the morning and made my way to the kitchen, the air smelled clean and crisp. I slowly ate breakfast, and my mind rifled through the endless possibilities of things I could do that day. It was summertime, so I had days on end without a care in the world. And best of all, there was no school!

After breakfast, I went into the computer room and what I discovered there instantly changed my life forever. I'm not sure how I stumbled across it, but once I opened it, it couldn't be unseen or undone. What I discovered was an email exchange between my father and a woman I'd never met before. The exchange made little sense to me, and I felt guilty about reading it. But for some reason, I couldn't stop myself.

Then all of a sudden, I read a few words that made the reality of the situation very clear. As I read and reread that fateful line, my ears began ringing, and I couldn't breathe. My dad was having an affair.

I quickly tried to close the email, and make it look like I'd never found it. But it was too late. I couldn't hide my panic. At that point, my mom came in and asked me what I was doing. I turned around to face her, and tears were rolling down my cheeks. Speechless, I pointed at the screen.

Afterward, I was so terrified about what I'd unearthed that I sat in my room—shaking. I was overwhelmed with feelings and emotions. I was consumed with so much that a twelve-year-old boy should not have to face on a typical summer day that just moments ago held so much hope and possibility. I desperately wanted to erase this whole experience. To hit pause and rewind. To go back to eating my breakfast and daydreaming my way through the day ahead of me.

But that's not how life works, right? I could never go back. I could never unsee what I saw. I could never be that typical twelve-year-old boy again. It's so crazy to think that one moment, one decision, could change the course of a person's life, but this is exactly what happened to me that day.

That morning I felt so many emotions that I had never felt before. I was angry at my dad and deeply saddened for my mom. On top of these heavy emotional burdens, I felt an immense amount of guilt. *What if I'd never looked at the computer that morning? What if I'd never clicked on the tab that held that email? Would things be different?* But most of all, I was scared about what would happen next. For the longest time I had this underlying fear that although my father loved our family so much and would do anything for us, the fact that he lacked love for himself would eventually lead to a moment I couldn't even comprehend.

It's not like things were perfect leading up to this moment. There were many nights I went to bed unsure of what was to come, but somehow, I knew this time was different. I knew this was one of those things that could not just be brushed off or shoved under the rug—that's what scared me the most. Written out plain as day, I knew that everything in my life up to this moment was about to be different. Our fragile reality, though already cracked, was now completely shattered, uprooted, and unearthed. That fear petrified my feet to the floor, and stopped my lungs from expanding, all I could do in that moment was feel my heart beating so hard I could hear it in my ears—my body's last effort to preserve what was, while I braced for my new reality.

Unfortunately, my deepest unspoken fears were realized the next morning. I woke up just in time to see my dad's taillights as he turned the corner.

He was gone. Forever.

Over the course of one day and one revelation of shattered trust, I lost my mentor, my idol, and the one man I looked to for everything in my life. I recalled the many nights I waited by the garage door at 10 pm for him to walk inside after work. Reality hit like a tsunami. The garage door was silenced—the door would never open in the same way again. He would never again walk through that door to find me waiting.

As the days wore on, I would hope against hope that he would change his mind and return home to us. We lived on a cul-de-sac and I would sit for hours looking through my window hoping he would pull up to the house, only to have my mom come in my room at 7 pm to pull the curtains down. She knew he wasn't coming back. And I suppose I did too deep down. But twelve-year-old boys need their dads, and my longing for him didn't go way just because he was no longer present in my life.

I desperately needed my dad.

Choosing Betterness, Not Bitterness

The weeks that followed seemed to drag on forever, as my little family tried to readjust to a new normal. We'd already gotten used to my dad's relationship with alcohol, but this affair just didn't make sense. I had so many questions, but no answers. *How could he have made this choice? How could he have let the alcohol take over to the point he'd have an affair? Were we so bad that we caused him to spiral out of control?*

I was only twelve, but all of a sudden, I was the man of the house. I felt like I had no one to turn to. My mother was so devastated that I knew not to go to her for support. So, I bottled it up. I internalized all of my questions, my fears, my self-loathing, and my guilt.

My childhood was over. I felt like it had been ripped away—stolen from me. It was taken without explanation. I could never really decide whether I was more sad or angry. My emotions changed like the seasons that followed. For months I would let the sadness get the best of me, that childlike innocence would creep in at the most unwelcome moments, for I was supposed to be a man now, but often I didn't feel I had the strength. And I shouldn't have had to. This is not the role of the child. But I took it on. I picked up the burden and carried it the best I knew how.

I think a lot of us share these types of traumatic life-altering experiences. Moments when the reality of the world come crashing down on our innocence—forcing us to grow up way too soon. It's sad. And it's a reflection on the adults around us. Families do what they know and if the family is not healthy—if each member has not done the soul-searching work of self-awareness and self-love, the effects spill out and over onto the children. This was my reality now. My life was forever changed because of the decisions of my parents. Decisions made out of dysfunction and self-loathing—learned thinking and behaviors likely learned from their own parents. And so, the cycle continued with me...

As the summer gave way to the fall and the shock had worn off, my anger would surge at the least opportune moments. I would feel red-hot, angry, pissed off, and furious that I was forced to be something I was not yet ready to be. Questions rattled around my mind, bouncing off the bones of my skull, leaving me with only more questions and no answers. The hopelessness, despair, and profound sadness that I did not know how to process lingered as I tried to make sense of this new life I was living—while doing my best to be the man my dad could not be for my mom and sister.

It was an unbearable weight at times. Just thinking of it now I can feel the heaviness of it all bearing down. No child should have to assume the burdens of their parents—reversing the roles of emotional support. But it occurs all too often, even today. Children will continue to be affected by the stunted emotional lives of their caregivers until they choose differently for themselves. The cycle will continue ad infinitum until someone chooses the difficult, yet life-transforming, work of self-reflection, self-awareness, and ultimately self-love.

You *can* choose differently. You *can* choose to stand up in the boat and change course. You can *choose* to be better.

The Choice

During the summer of unraveling, I discovered a stash of my dad's alcohol in my closet after he moved out. Within just a few short weeks, the only thing left of him in the house was a few cans of beer that taunted me after I found them hidden under an old shirt.

At first, I was outraged. But then I just stood for a moment and contemplated my next move. *Perhaps the beer would ease my pain? Maybe it would help me feel close to my dad again, just for a moment.* Maybe, maybe, maybe...?

And so, I cracked a beer open and as the carbonation fizzed, I breathed in the familiar smell—which was briefly comforting. I brought the can to my lips, but I stopped when I heard a voice in my head, as clear as day: *Do I want to be the person I'm about to become? Do I want to follow in my dad's footsteps? Do I want to hurt the rest of my family the way he hurt me?*

Or do I want to be better than him?

I can't tell you how angry I was that I was being asked to choose, when all I wanted was to feel better. Then I looked down and envisioned the children I would have someday looking up at me—tugging at my pant legs and wanting to play. And just like that—my choice was clear.

As I cracked every beer open and poured them out—watching the contents spiral and foam around the drain, a calm feeling came over me. It was like a sign that this chapter of my life was over. No more watching my dad drink, no more watching my mom try to save him, no more cleaning up after him. We were done, and I'd made the decision to be the man he couldn't be.

That day, I chose betterness for the first time. Betterness isn't the easy route, as it requires self-awareness and a deep love for yourself. It's facing your soul and understanding that you can love yourself *through* your growth. Betterness is forgiving yourself, breaking family cycles, and not allowing moments of adversity to change or dictate who you are at your core.

Putting that can of beer down and choosing betterness in my life created an intensely profound moment. I made the conscious decision to live a sober life that would enable me to write my own story. In that moment, I decided to become a father and husband that wouldn't ever leave his family, and I understood that my life had deep meaning and purpose. If I hadn't chosen betterness, I would have repeated all the mistakes my dad made. Instead, I stood up in the boat. I broke the cycle. I forever changed the course of my life and the lives of my family to come.

This experience was especially powerful because somehow, I had the awareness to put the alcohol down. At such a young age I already knew the intoxicating effects were temporary and a life filled with drunken days is not a life at all—in fact, it's like a slow, excruciating death.

Somehow, I knew.

I saw how alcohol affected my dad and how that spilled over onto my entire family. Somehow, I knew how easy it would be to repeat his self-destructive choices. Somehow, I knew that bitterness would be easier than betterness. Somehow, I knew I *had* to make the better choice.

To this day I really don't understand where this "knowing" came from. Even adults struggle with listening to their inner voice and following their gut. This lack of self-awareness is what causes people to get stuck in the cycle of bitterness, instead of realizing that a better life is contingent on constant growth. Choosing betterness is harder, but it's the only decision that results in self-love.

If I'd held onto that bitterness, I can assure you of one thing: I wouldn't be where I am in my life today.

While I was staring at that beer, I felt desperately alone. In that moment, I wanted to stay in that isolation and live in my pain. In that moment I felt like choosing the path that my dad had chosen. I felt like drinking would somehow connect me to him. I see now that this was magical thinking. Drinking, isolation and continued dysfunction would only connect me to the sick parts of my dad. I so desperately wanted him to be something he simply could not be for himself or for me. This revelation was devastating to the twelve-year-old me.

We've all had moments in our lives when it feels like every sad song on the radio is playing directly to us. On those days, it seems like there's no hope to be had. But after the wallowing and self-pity wear off, we have to choose to get up, dust ourselves off, and keep moving. And in those moments, we learn what it means to need self-love. In those moments, if we allow ourselves to truly feel the depths of our feelings, we bravely step onto the path toward that great need.

The First Step

Since my journey to self-understanding and self-love began, I've been sharing stories with others about how I chose to make positive choices in the face of adversity—not just one time, but for the rest of my life. And here's what I've learned time and time again:

Choosing betterness is the first step toward self-love.

When you make the hard decision to do better and be a better person, it helps you spread love more abundantly. Once you make that choice for yourself and you become clear on who you are and why you exist in this world, no one will have the power to steer you away from your life's goals and purpose.

Betterness means knowing and trusting that we are enough. Period. Exclamation point. Betterness is having full confidence that we are equipped and empowered with all the tools we need to overcome hardship with grace, gratitude, and forgiveness. Too many times, we look at others to fill roles and answer questions about who we are. But when we choose betterness, we choose constant, unending self-improvement. It's a lifelong choice, and it can be made in an instant. You don't have to clean up your life first to make this choice. By simply making the choice toward betterness, your life will clean up naturally. You can start today and see the light that tomorrow will bring.

When we get caught up in a painful situation, our todays become yesterdays, and we start losing sight of our tomorrows. Being bitter about your past will hold you back, even if the bitterness started recently. You have no way to change your past; all you can do is control your actions in the present and the future. Don't dwell on what you can't change, but focus on how you can improve. Practice forgiveness in yourself, and offer it to others.

We're all human, and I believe we all do the best we can with the coping skills and life experiences we have at the time. Inevitably, we will make mistakes, so give yourself permission to forgive yourself for them, learn from them, move on, and do better moving forward. You are—and always have been—worthy of that kind of acceptance and forgiveness.

One of the biggest questions I hear from my clients is: *How do I forget the girl or guy who's no longer in my life?* People are struggling to move on from people, situations, and feelings that limit their potential. If a person is no longer in your life for whatever reason, dwelling on it will prevent betterness. Everyone who touches your life has a purpose, so don't mistake a lesson for a lifelong love. Accept what it is that they were in your life to teach you, thank them—offer gratitude, forgiveness, and love—and release them. You too will then be free.

It's one thing to be present with people in your life, but it's quite another to be present with yourself. It's hard for most people to understand how to be present with themselves, and some people can't fathom being alone. In fact, some people feel like they need a plethora of things and people surrounding them all the time.

If you're someone who hates being alone, try to change your mindset. Instead of filling your time with distractions, ask yourself: *Why can't I stand being alone? Is it because I'm afraid I'll be missing out? Is it because I don't want to disappoint someone? Is it because I have an image to uphold?*

If you answered yes to any of these questions, let me offer you a piece of advice that I was offered during my self-love journey:

Distractions don't allow you to heal.

If you have wounds, tend to them, nourish them, and let them heal. The process of healing isn't an overnight endeavor. In fact, if that is what you are hoping for, I'm sure there's a get-rich-quick scheme out there that will convince you otherwise, along with making a million dollars by tomorrow. I pray you don't choose that route and instead take note on the following: Invest time *with* yourself and *by* yourself. The mirror doesn't define you and neither does a sour relationship. It's all in your life for a reason. It's all learning. It's all a catalyst propelling you toward your self-love awakening. You alone can put the pieces back together. Accept yourself. You are better for having gone through every single experience in your life. Even the most painful ones. Often *because* of the most painful ones.

We are so quick to mask our wounds not because we don't want to face other people, but because we don't want to face ourselves. Therefore, instead of spending time with ourselves, journaling, listening to music in peace, going outside in nature, or taking a drive down the beach, to slow things down just a bit so we can process what's really going on, we choose to allow anything and everything under the sun to temporarily distract us from our own truth. Remember, ignoring a problem allows the wound to fester, spread, and steal your peace. You're in control of your journey and you can't live with open wounds forever.

Trust me when I say I'm not perfect. I've also dealt with self-hatred. When I had these feelings, I didn't feel worthy, so I responded to my circumstances with bitterness. Before I realized there's an infinite amount of love inside myself to give to the world, I felt empty—like I needed somebody close to me to survive. Like so many other people, I struggled with blame and self-loathing anytime a relationship didn't work out. Even though I knew I wanted betterness, I let other people's actions spiral me back into bitterness.

It took me many years to connect this self-loathing and need for other people to my own experiences. Even though I chose betterness at a young age, I still struggled for years because I didn't fully let go of the bitterness.

Summary of Betterness

The first step to choosing betterness is releasing bitterness, which means we release all expectations from people. This step includes releasing the ways you expect others to be, and what you expect them to do. The next step involves never letting circumstances change who you fundamentally at the core of your soul.

Selflovology Tips for Betterness

- Retell your own story in a positive way. When you want to vent, reinvent the way you look at it.

- Come up with five reminders of the things you'll do every single day that make you happy.

- Remember that bullying is about them, not you.

- Practice thankfulness, even at your lowest points.

- To counter bitterness, imagine being the person that hurt you, and consider how full of self-hatred he or she must be.

- Remind yourself that you deserve better by using positive self-talk.

Chapter 2

Obstacles That Prevent Self-Love

"If you run into a wall, don't turn around and give up. Figure out how to climb it, go through it, or work around it."

Michael Jordan

Moving toward self-love can be impossible if obstacles aren't acknowledged and met head on. Is it worth it to fit in if everyone loves you except yourself? I'll answer for you: absolutely not. At the end of the day, or at the end of a life, nothing matters more than how well you loved—others and yourself. And the truth is you cannot love well without first learning to love yourself fully and completely without condition.

If you want to grow toward this level of self-love, you have to obliterate the awareness and knowledge of this strange dynamic holding each of us down. Why do we care so much about what others think or feel about us? Does it really matter at the end of the day?

Imagine that you're a young child, and you have an empty box. You see the empty box, and your eyes light up with anticipation. You're free to fill it with whatever you like, so you carefully pick out your most prized possessions and put them into the box with much care and attention—looking at and smiling at each treasure as you lower it into the box. I can feel the thrill of this even now. I recall moments like this as a child when I had a simple yet very important task like choosing my absolute favorite toys to take in a backpack on vacation.

The choice seemed like magic.

As you get older, the box becomes less prized and treasured. You no longer look at the box with the magical eyes of a child who sees the endless possibilities. You are older now; the world has colored your life and your perspective in myriad ways.

Now it's just a box.

It gets filled with very little care and attention. It has become a junk-drawer rather than a box of prized possessions. The box gets piled up with all kinds of things that people bring you, and it eventually gets overcrowded and worn down. The things you once cherished in childhood are now lost somewhere at the bottom—forgotten and overlooked. You can no longer access the magical things that you once loved. They are buried beneath the mundane and ordinary. The box no longer represents you and all of life's possibilities. It's simply a box of "stuff."

As time goes on, the box is a hindrance—not a treasure. It is overloaded and spilling out with "things" that truly do not matter to us. We see the box and we know it is no longer a picture of us, but somehow can't let it go. Instead, we carry it around. The weight of the box and its meaningless contents is like an albatross around our necks. We don't know how to release it, so we live our lives figuring out ways to continue carrying it.

The box is a metaphor for other people's opinions we encounter and take on as truth as we grow up and experience the world. It is a symbol of all of the junk that we have collected along the way that is holding us down—holding us hostage—keeping us from achieving our life's true purpose.

In order to move toward self-awareness and self-love, we must completely dismantle the box. We must sit with it and take a hard look at the contents. This can be uncomfortable, but it must be done so the box does not fill up again with meaningless clutter.

Take time to sit with your box. Look carefully at each element within it. Ask yourself if it is serving you and your life. If the answer is no, release it. Once you have cleaned your box and it is only filled with items that lift you up and serve your purpose in life—you must guard it because I can guarantee no one else will protect and defend it.

Moving forward, be selective about what you take on and place within your box. Remember the image of the wide-eyed child—carefully and intentionally filling the box with only the most cherished and valued possessions. Don't let others' perceptions become unnecessary weight in your box. They will only cover up and hide your truest self and prevent you from becoming all that you are meant to be.

When I first decided to take an honest look at my box, the experience was quite harsh. It was kind of like going into a closet two weeks after you've already been home from vacation, only to see your suitcase half opened with all the dirty clothes still in it, screaming at you from the rooftops to be thrown into the laundry.

What I did come to learn though was that I could no longer tip toe in order to create a significant splash in my life. I had to unbox who I hadn't been willing to forgive—which was ultimately myself. I sat and took a hard and painful look at my own box—bowing and cracking at the seams. I forgave myself for my past relationships, my business failures, negative thoughts about my body, and I finally felt like I could breathe again.

I came back to life—my life—and I realized my worth and that my life held great value and was extremely worth living.

When I committed to my own process of unboxing, one of the very first hard looks I had to take was at my childhood trauma. This reckoning was one of the most difficult experiences of my life—in many ways it was more excruciating than the actual trauma. Looking at and examining the pain of your childhood as an adult is an experience like no other. You are older, more mature, and you've seen and experienced more of the world and how it works. You have seen life outside of the tiny bubble that you lived within as a child.

It's heartbreaking. It cracks you open. On top of severe emotional turmoil, I experienced actual physical pain in my body. The mind and body never truly forget. They keep score.

I unpacked my trauma by making peace with the fact that no one is perfect. I was raised by two very imperfect beings. I recognized and acknowledged that my parents did the best job they could with the knowledge they had at the time.

After all, it's one thing to take care of yourself, let alone raising children while working a job and trying to still hold some level of sanity all at the same time. There was no more blaming them, my upbringing, what I witnessed, or who they were or weren't.

I had to accept what was and forgive my parents for not being all that I needed them to be. I felt sadness and compassion for them because as an adult I understood that they were not able to be anything other than what they were. They simply did not know how. They were fighting their own battles and living from a place of their own pain. My parents simply did not have the tools to do better. I just happened to have a front row seat. I think this is a common thread in many people's stories. How could it not be... there is no parenting manual and just because one becomes a parent doesn't cancel out and heal their own deep childhood wounds.

Unboxing my own childhood trauma meant taking full accountability and having full self-awareness that I am now in control of my life and if I want things to change, I need to change. It's no longer about anyone else. I had to practice radical forgiveness and grace—for myself and for my parents.

Now take some time to unpack your box. What's in it? What do you need to keep carrying? What can you simply remove from your box, so you can more quickly move toward your dream life? The choice is yours. Embrace that power; it will set you free to walk your own unique path in the world.

Before we can even walk or talk, we are color-coded and stamped with labels that aren't conducive to becoming an individual with unique gifts. Words are spoken over us from the earliest age and they contain very little truth about who we truly are. We absorb and take on these words and roles that others have created for us and we forge ahead—leaving our true selves behind. It's quite sad really.

And it could be so different if only people understood the damage being done—the lives being lost.

Great strength, faith, and stubborn resolve are required to reconnect to that truest part of yourself and remain on course toward your purpose and goals. I hope that's why you're reading this book, and why you want to begin the journey to self-love.

Selflovology is about slowly breaking down the obstacles that cause people pain—starting with yourself.

By understanding self-love and releasing your own barriers, you're able to help others do the same. Self-love grows and cultivates:

• Greater expressions of compassion, forgiveness, and grace.

• Abundance—rather than scarcity and envy.

• An understanding that the only time we should look down at someone is if we're reaching down to help them up.

When you are compassionate towards yourself, you'll find compassion towards others. For example, you'll be keenly aware of the fact that everyone is doing the best they can with the tools they have at the time. It's not an excuse for wrong or dysfunctional behavior, but if you truly think about it... if they knew better, they would do better. If they knew different, they would do different. Recognizing this allows you to see what's going on with people below the surface. You can now see when tough situations arrive with someone else's actions, it's not about you and it's about where they are within themselves.

When you examine and release your own barriers you'll begin to come from a place of abundance versus scarcity, envy, or jealousy.

Releasing your own mask enables you to understand that the goal is to be better than who you were yesterday, not spending your precious time and life comparing, being jealous of, or trying to "win" a battle with someone who may not even know you exist.

Self-love will encourage you to help the people with whom you're surrounded. You will begin to understand that there's room for everyone to be healthy, to succeed, to love and be loved, and to accomplish all they desire. You are no longer there for others only when they are weak, upset, or sick. You are now able to be there for them when they succeed, become fulfilled, and are creating their best life because of their new found self-love.

It's contagious. The more you work on your own self-love, the more others will see the changes within you and they will desperately want what you have. You will be helping others by helping yourself. It's a beautiful outpouring. Self-love begets further self-love within yourself and in those around you.

Selflovology is all about helping people get up, so they can break down the walls that prevent self-love.

Learning how to break down barriers is one of the toughest steps toward achieving limitless self-love. For years, I struggled with trying to love myself, while also making room in my mind for how people thought I should behave. Believing that "what other people say doesn't matter" is easier said than done.

In the end, it's very human to want to feel connected and loved. Here's the difference: When you set yourself free from holding onto expectations—of yourself and others—you allow yourself to attract people who appreciate and celebrate your uniqueness, rather than trying to convince yourself that your beliefs are unattainable.

Trust me, the journey to self-love is hard work. But it is the most important work you will ever do. I'll be the first to admit that committing to a life of self-love presented many challenges. It wasn't all butterflies and rainbows—quite the opposite in fact. It can be dark and lonely, and it can bring up parts of yourself that you never knew existed. But this hard, introspective work is the only way to the other side. You can't go around it. You must go straight through.

An Easy Target

One of the personal barriers I had to overcome was the wrath I faced for being different during high school. Imagine: I was 13, and my dad had just abandoned my family. I had a single mom. I was tall and too thin. Within a few short weeks, it became clear to me that it wasn't cool to be different in high school—at least not the kind of different I was.

Several boys my age saw me as an easy target, and from there, there was no stopping them. For months, they rallied together and made my life a living hell. They would belittle me, call me names, and throw things at me. However, I never retaliated, which fueled their fire even more.

As time went on, I started dreading going to school. I knew I'd never find peace because I didn't fit in. It would have been so much easier for me to cave in, rally with them, and find someone else to pick on. But I just couldn't get myself to fold my hand like that. I remained calm, took the abuse, and didn't let it change my character.

Eventually, the bullying became so severe I decided to change high schools, hoping I'd have a fresh start. Once again, I had no luck. I was the new kid, and I wasn't into partying. Again, I was the perfect target.

This time, my tires were slashed because I wouldn't conform. But I didn't want to give into peer pressure. I couldn't bring myself to be something I was not, and the bullying became so severe that I received several death threats.

Grasp that concept for a second: Other teens were threatening me with knives and guns because they felt I was different. Part of me so wished I could be normal, but it wasn't in my DNA. What does that mean anyway... normal? Teenagers were setting the standard for normalcy, and I didn't fit the bill.

After a while, I refused to go back to school because I was afraid of what might happen to me if I didn't conform.

My mom finally agreed to let me be home-schooled. Biweekly, I met with a teacher to go over my homework packets, but other than that, I spent most of my time alone.

My sheer stubbornness to be who I was left me isolated and alone. Many times, I wondered if not being able to fit in meant there was really something wrong with me. I wondered: *Why is it so horrible that I don't party, cuss, or drink, and that I treat my teachers with respect?* I couldn't comprehend that my lack of rebellion had left me at the mercy of the cool kids. It would have been so easy to break down and conform. Sadly, we see this happening to kids every day. They stuff down and hide who they truly are to take on the look or personality of kids who are empty and void of feelings and compassion.

During the summer before my senior year, my mom encouraged me to try again. At that point, I was more than weary about attending another high school. *Wouldn't it make me an even easier target to be the kid who'd been to every high school in the area, and had no friends?* I was the textbook definition of an outcast.

Nevertheless, I agreed to give it another chance. This time, I went to a school in a less affluent area, and something amazing happened: I didn't get bullied. When I came home, I was so excited. This school didn't have cliques like the others. The popular kids hung out with the special-needs kids. The jocks hung out with the theater crowd. Everyone was in harmony. I was perplexed, and tried to decipher why this school was so different.

Later, I realized there was a sense of understanding and acceptance because this school brought together people of various backgrounds. Everyone understood that each individual had challenges and barriers in their personal lives.

Due to the sheer diversity of the student population, I encountered more compassion, understanding, and equality. Through this new experience I realized I wasn't crazy—I simply didn't let my circumstances change my personality. This realization stole the power from the bullies that wanted to break my spirit. I let go of my fear, overcame my distaste for school, and was a happy teenage boy by the time I graduated from high school.

This experience was very powerful, and provided innumerable lessons. A few of the most impactful:

1. **Your beliefs are good enough - whatever they are.**

   You don't have to become someone you're not. You don't have to hide. You are perfect just the way you are. Stand in your power, and allow yourself to shine. By upholding your standards and your loyalty to yourself, you'll be able to keep your head held up high. If you conform to something you don't believe in, you'll be left feeling unfulfilled.

2. **You shouldn't take other people's actions toward you personally.**

   Resistance and upheaval are natural parts of finding and following your path. Allow them to pass over you, and don't get caught up in other people's emotions.

   What other people think of you is none of your business. Other people's opinions shouldn't concern you if you're following the path you believe is right. This is your life—not theirs. So, you should feel free to do as you wish.

3. **You can never know what other people are experiencing, thinking, or feeling.**

   Realize that everyone is fighting their own personal battles within themselves. Therefore, you can't predict or control their actions. Instead, focus on controlling your own. You know you, so let that be enough.

4. **Loving yourself knows no barriers.**

   Learn to stand by your own side, lock arms with yourself, and never let life's barriers take you somewhere you don't want to go.

On my journey to being better, my experiences in high school were simply obstacles. When we're going through a trying time, the simple ways we'll bless each other's lives isn't always clear.

Even today, I'm still learning from these experiences. Years later, one of the boys who bullied me in high school actually asked me to coach him about self-love. What a beautiful full-circle moment that was.

The Octogenarian Bully

When I started this journey of unpacking my box and sharing that with the world as a way of living and thriving versus surviving, I didn't even know what self-love was. Now, I realize I can discipline myself to be focused on positivity.

It's important to share the message that you will see your dream through if you become better, attract better and stay focused. This lesson became especially clear one day when the most amazing yet sad thing happened to me.

I was at a local coffee shop, and it was so packed that there was nowhere to sit. But I noticed there was a chair open with a group of about eight seniors. So I asked them if I could sit there, and ended up beside a beautiful 86-year-old woman and her husband. They go there every day to have coffee and visit with their group of friends.

When we started talking, they asked me what I do, and of course, the topic of self-love came up. To my surprise, the lovely lady I was sitting next to opened up and quietly told me that she needed self-love in her life because another woman in her group had been bullying her for years. Even though she chose to see her every day, this bully kept telling her that she was ugly and worthless, and that her husband didn't love her.

Soon, tears welled up in this woman's eyes as I tightly grasped her hand and told her she was beautiful.

I talked to her about how to love herself more, and her husband and I both asked her why she was allowing this bully to add such negativity to her life. As I was talking to this beautiful yet insecure woman, I could also see the bitterness in the bully.

I have to admit it: I was shocked that what I was hearing reminded me so much of high school, and I was sad that it was happening to women in their late 80s. You really can learn from everyone.

It really was a stark reminder that you're surrounded by other people's opinions of yourself—from the moment you're born until the moment you die. Remember, you can choose self-love today and every day.

Self-hatred shows up in a lot of ways, and it's especially poignant in bullying situations like this one. The woman who was being bullied didn't have any self-love. Every day, she was choosing to subject herself to these mean, nasty words and actions.

But the bully didn't have self-love either. She made herself feel better by belittling this woman who was supposed to be her friend. If she loved herself, she wouldn't want to hurt others to lift herself up.

Summary of Obstacles

Remember, bullying is one of many obstacles that will try to distract you from the life you desire. There will always be someone in your life trying to stop you from achieving your goals—but only if you let them. If you remove the obstacle, you begin to see that anything and everything is possible, but it takes discipline and self-love.

Throughout your journey, you're going to encounter people who want to harm you or tear you down. It could be the person closest to you, or someone you'd never expect. Regardless of who you are, you're going to deal with somebody judging you or putting down your character. In the digital age we now live in, it's even easier, and it may be someone you don't even know.

Again, you have a choice.

You can choose to overcome all the obstacles that prevent self-love. Don't count yourself out before you count yourself in. Accept your circumstances, stop wasting your energy complaining, and start doing something. Be aware of conversations that are meaningless, draining, or negative, and prepare for obstacles before they occur. Barriers take many shapes, and they span over the course of our lives. But if we can train ourselves to recognize and dismantle them, we will be free.

There's nothing you can't do if you want it badly enough. The only person who can stop you is yourself. Take solace in knowing that you are—and always have been—in the driver's seat of your life. If you see an obstacle ahead of you, take an exit, circumvent the barrier, move forward with self-awareness and peace, and learn to appreciate your ability to know which issues are worth acknowledging.

Obstacles That Prevent Self-Love

Remember, what people say about you isn't true unless you believe it. You're on the right path. Trust in yourself, and nothing will stand in your way.

Selflovology Tips for Obstacles

- List your obstacles. What's holding you back?

- From your list, select the Top 5 biggest challenges. After you mentally overcome them, burn the list.

- Figure out what box you are trying to fit into and why.

- Find a mentor or friend who can help you work through some of your obstacles.

- Use the people who are against you and the roadblocks in your way to propel you forward with more determination.

- The next time you're in an uncomfortable situation, think about why you're uncomfortable, and change your assumptions.

- When you face an obstacle, choose betterness instead of bitterness. Know they're making you powerful.

- When you are struggling to see the benefits of a specific challenge, write down 3 things you're thankful for.

- Remember, hurt people hurt people. The people who cause you pain only do so because they don't love themselves.

Chapter 3

Being Present

> *"In the stillness of your presence ... You look
> beyond the veil of form and separation. This is
> the realization of oneness. This is love."*
>
> **Eckhart Tolle**

As humans, we have an innate need to be part of a community. We thrive on human interaction, but in this day and age, a true human connection has become increasingly rare. Blame it on the internet, on how fast-paced our world has become, or on a money-driven mentality. Whatever you believe the reason is, we can all agree that our interactions with others have changed over the last few decades.

As a result, something has been compromised that everyone values: being physically, mentally, and emotionally present with other people. Think about the last time you were able to be powerfully present with someone, without multitasking and being distracted (usually by your phone).

We are also wired as deeply spiritual beings meant to know and understand ourselves. If you are struggling to connect with others on a personal level, I can guarantee it is because you are not taking the time to connect with yourself. This disassociation with yourself leads to survival-mode, burn-out, and countless issues that keep you from being truly able to connect with others.

Self-connection is a building block of interpersonal connection. We cannot give what we do not have. We cannot pour out into others if our own well is dry.

If it's been awhile since you've intentionally spent time with yourself, don't worry. It's not your fault, and you're certainly not the only one. We all struggle with this.

There are so many things screaming for our attention these days and society doesn't put value on spending time in self-reflection. We have bought into the notion that faster is better. We have been tricked to think the busier we are the better we are. We live under the tyranny of the urgent.

Let me just tell you all of this is a flat out lie.

We must make time for ourselves. We can be successful in business and successful in life. It's not one or the other. We *can* have it all if we make ourselves a priority.

Once we ourselves are healthy and self-connected, the connections with others will become second nature. We will be able to pour into others, and we will be balanced enough to really see and hear them. Our pace will slow, and our interactions with others will be more rich and meaningful. We will refine our relationships by being fully and completely present. Our advice will come from a place of deep calm rather than chaos, and the art of listening will return to our conversations.

Canned Responses

Think about this example: You walk into work, and your secretary gives you a canned greeting: "Good morning. How are you?"

Most of us probably give an equally canned response: "I'm good. How are you?" We don't even think about what was actually being asked. We've been programmed to respond in a generic way. We know the standards of conduct, so we oblige without giving our actions a second thought.

But what has this programming done to us as humans who long to be present, have intimate connections, and be part of a community? It's trained us to disconnect, and focus only on the superficial in conversation—to hear and respond rather than to listen, digest, and continue the conversation. It's become robotic—automated.

In this chapter, we're going to explore how to unlearn these habits, and why being powerfully present is monumentally important for mastering our own self-love.

Here's the short version: We need to learn to be fully present with ourselves before we are able to engage with others in meaningful ways that lead to self-awareness and self-love.

Type of Presence

Before we take some time to learn how to reconnect with ourselves, let's take a closer look at how presence (or the lack thereof) can impact our relationships. Divorce rates are still hovering at around 50%, and while there are many reasons for this alarming statistic, I firmly believe that lack of presence is one of them.

In order to foster healthy, mutually fulfilling relationships, we need to become more self-aware about how we choose to interact. During the next conversation you have with someone you love, be aware of the types of things you say. Are you simply asking the same old questions, but don't really care about the response? Or are you emotionally engaging the person you're talking to and having a fulfilling conversation?

The next thing you have to ask yourself is: How am I speaking to this person? What tone of voice am I using? Am I allowing them to fully speak their minds, or am I hastily adding to the conversation?

Oftentimes, we're so accustomed to being half-present during conversations that it can be uncomfortable to tune in and be powerfully present. Some people find direct eye contact and intentional listening intimidating, especially if they have been starving their need for reciprocal presence for a long time.

By becoming more in tune with the ways you interact with others, you'll learn some very important things:

- How much time and energy you're giving each person in your life.

- Who is worthy of this time and energy.

- How to be aware of your own need for reciprocal presence in the people you decide are worthy of it.

Engaging Minds

To become fully present, one of the first lessons you need to learn is that presence goes beyond simply being with someone in the same place at the same time. Being present means engaging with someone else's spirit and mind.

I discovered a powerful depiction of this concept in a painting I once saw in an art museum in Los Angeles. Two people's faces were close together, and there was light coming from each of their foreheads, which was connected in an explosion of light in the middle. Instead of hairlines, they had hinges, and their skulls were hanging open. Words, emotions, light, energy, love, and passion flowed out of the tops of their heads. To this day, I still envision this painting when I think about being powerfully present with someone.

In order to foster this type of presence, find ways to be fulfilled during conversations that encourage and uplift the people you're with. To move away from multiple distractions and become present in intimate moments, you need both practice and vigor, presence doesn't just naturally happen, it is intentionally created.

Increasing your awareness, attention, and connection in conversation allows you to:

- Create clear intentions with the person you're interacting with.

- Delve deeper than your canned responses.

- Talk about things that will fill your primal need to make an intimate connection, in a world that's often too busy and distracted to forage these moments.

The challenge isn't usually creating an intention—it's communicating it via your body language and verbal language. Deciding what you want is valuable, but without communicating that clearly and specifically, the person you're interacting with will not know what you desire or how you are feeling.

We are now living in a society where "I'm good" is accepted as a response for the question "How are you?" Most people take this canned response at face value and don't seek more information about the other person's true well-being.

It's a break-down of communication on both sides. "How are you?" has become rushed and sterile. We rarely look the other person in the eyes and truly seek to know how they are at the deepest levels. At the same time, our "I'm good" style responses are diversions from what we really need to express.

Skimming the surface of interconnection will get us nowhere.

I promise you, we can do better. The next time you are with someone, look them in the eyes when you're speaking with them. I know you're thinking that might be weird, but let's face it... you drove 30 miles to be with them, not the wall or your phone that you're with 24-7. Focus on listening to understand versus listening to respond. That will enable you to respond in a deeper manner versus responding with a typical answer they could've come up with themselves. And most importantly, it gives you time to breathe and sip on your first Shirley temple since 1995. Who wouldn't want that?

Everything starts and ends with the self as discussed earlier. You have to be committed to a daily practice of self-connection in order to grow your capacity to connect with others on the deepest and most fulfilling levels.

When this daily practice begins to bear fruit, you will project light and opportunities for a connection. Imagine you are a lighthouse for a moment. A lighthouse serves as a beacon of light in the dark distance that brings people back home. If you live your life as a metaphorical light house—you are creating endless opportunities to bring people back home to themselves. They may not get to it right away, but their true being is always trying to get back to the light. When you operate in the world, it should always be out of a place of light in the effort to bring people home.

What a powerful visual. It's absolutely stunning like the painting in the Los Angeles museum.

A lighthouse—shining bright healthy beams of light flowing into the darkness and droves of people turning from their old ways to soak up and follow the light...

Be the lighthouse.

They will find you. And in the process, they will find themselves.

The Missing Key

It may seem like a daunting task to learn to be present with yourself. Isn't that ironic? We live our whole lives with ourselves, and often-times, we know more about everyone else than we do about our-selves. In my journey to finding my own self-love, I found this par-ticular topic to be one of the hardest to understand.

It's easy to say, "Well, I already know myself. I know when I'm hungry and when I'm happy. I know what I like and what I don't like. What am I missing?" The key to learning to be present with yourself is learning to be in tune with what you're thinking and feeling at all times. This type of awareness and connection to yourself goes far beyond your immediate primal needs for food, water, sleep, etc.

Primal needs will always be met. We don't have to worry about them or overthink the process. When you are hungry, you will seek out food. When you are thirsty, water will be your only thought. When your body is so tired that it needs rest, you will lie down and rest.

It's our emotional selves that need to be taught to express. We are all born with innate emotional needs and the capacity to express those needs, but somewhere along the way we stop articulating these desires. When we are young, we easily express when we are afraid, we freely share when we feel sad, and we don't think twice about this expression.

It's like breathing.

The older we get, the more closed off our feelings become. Expression is not safe. We can't control the outcomes. It's too vulnerable, so we either shut the feelings down completely or we stop expressing. Both are toxic. We have to rewrite this narrative for ourselves and for generations to come.

Learning Backwards

In a sense, becoming more present with yourself often requires learning backwards. In other words, you must first look at your actions or habits to become more self-aware, since they're the outward expressions of your thoughts. Then you must break down your actions and understand why you choose to act the way you do. After you understand the emotions that are driving your actions, you must further learn to reflect on why certain actions trigger certain emotions.

Envision each behavior like a rose: You must peel back each layer to get to the core of the causes of your actions and understand yourself. In essence, you're learning backwards. One at a time, you peel the layers of petals back to discover what gave it life to begin with: the pollen in the middle. Once you get to the center, you'll understand how everything else subsequently occurred.

While somewhat time-consuming at first, this exercise will better equip and empower you to become more present with yourself so you can start learning forward. Once you learn how to backtrack, you're able to gain a deeper understanding of what drives your emotions, your actions, and your thoughts. Then you'll be able to be aware of yourself—your emotions and your feelings— during each moment of your day.

By dismantling your actions, you've taught yourself your tendencies, your strengths, your weaknesses, and your pain points. With this increased awareness, you're able to control your actions and thoughts in a different way. Instead of reflecting, you're able to stop yourself and use your newfound self-awareness to talk through situations with yourself. You can also learn to respond, rather than react.

Over time and with mindful practice, the two parts of yourself—the emotional being and the physical being will be brought back into beautiful union as they were always meant to be.

Facets

One thing you must understand about learning how to become powerfully present is that every individual is multifaceted. Furthermore, you must understand why each of those facets of your personality shows up at certain times. Where did each one come from, and how does it protect or hinder you in your life?

Each facet exists for a reason, usually because it's served you in some part of your life. However, if you don't learn to speak the same language as each facet, you'll end up having a power struggle.

Personally, I've learned that four very distinct facets exist inside of me. Each one comes out in certain situations, and all of them are tied to my life experiences. They are:

1. **The Overachiever**

   This part of my personality is never satisfied. He always wants me to do more, achieve more, and cast my vision bigger and wider. He's been both a positive and negative force in my life.

   On one hand, he challenges me and is a huge reason why I am where I am in my life today. He pushes me, tells me there is more to be done, and lets me be honest. Oftentimes, he tells me there's no such thing as enough. He's the reason I overcame my dad leaving and the bullying that followed. In essence, he's my powerhouse.

   However, he also steals my victories from me because he always wants to set the bar higher. He makes it difficult for me to give myself credit for my achievements.

   When I weigh the two facets of the overachiever in me, it's clear that he takes more than he gives. I want to feel my victories. It is in this that I am propelled forward toward more and more success.

   It's like positive vs. negative self-talk. My overachiever speaks within me in both ways. The negative talk shouts that I am never enough. This is not a sustainable way to live. Conversely, the positive facet of my overachiever speaks kindly and lifts me up—allowing me to see just how powerful I truly am.

As I recognize this, it's now up to me to choose which voice I listen to. This is hard work. Daily work. The choice is not always simple.

2. The Soft Spot

The Soft Spot always chooses to see the good in people, and he's quick to blindly believe in them. As you can imagine, he tends to get hurt. Oftentimes, he's overly trusting and chooses not to use practical reasoning in friendships.

I've learned he comes from my innate belief that all people are good. He loves all people, and truly believes that no one will do anything to hurt someone else. He's been a huge influence on my ability to relate to people and a major driving force in why I've chosen the life path I have.

However, he's cost me a great deal of time and money, by putting trust in people who don't always have my best interests at heart.

I have had to learn to tamper my soft spot with experience and rational reasoning. It is good to trust people. However, it is also good to listen to your past experiences and to learn to listen to your instincts. Your gut will never lie. It will always steer you toward the truth. Listen.

3. The Shadow

Whenever I was close to veering away from what the Shadow thought my life should look like, he filled me with doubt and fear.

He comes from a place of external expectations and lack of self-belief.

When I was younger, the Shadow taught me that believing in myself was dangerous, and that I should be afraid of the world and the people in it. He was my protector, and he always tried to prevent me from getting hurt or lost as I grew up.

He's still there now as a grown man. I like to think that I have more control over him now than he has over me. But I don't really know for sure. He comes and goes. My awareness of him helps, but like the other facets I have to fight daily to let him know that *I* am in control and to keep him in check.

4. The Superhero

This facet is larger than life, positive, and ready to conquer the world. As you can imagine, the Superhero and Overachiever are very close friends. He gives me passion, and drives me to explore as many avenues of life as possible. He is fearless and courageous, and always full of life.

The Superhero is my own personal cheerleader. He's always proud of me, optimistic, and ready to go. He sprouted from my youth like a mental form of my mother. He protects my dreams, and always tells me nothing is impossible. Many times, I've counted on him to give me the strength to keep going.

But while he's immensely powerful, he can also cause me to move too fast. I've had to learn how to curb his enthusiasm in certain situations, because he's like a kid in a candy store. He wants me to move in every direction at once.

Learning Their Languages

By mastering my own presence and self-awareness, I had to learn to speak the unique language of each one of my facets. They each have their own emotions, their own positives and negatives, and their own triggers. Until I figured out how to learn backwards, I didn't understand who my facets are and how they show up in my life.

By learning why they're living inside of me, I was able to become aware of the presence of each of them. Today, I'm able to avoid power struggles between my facets, so I can harness and unleash each of their positives to help me. Meanwhile, I can remain aware of their drawbacks, and find ways to curb their dark sides.

For example, when writing this book, which facets do you think took the forefront of my mind? You guessed it: the Overachiever and the Superhero. Once I decided to take the plunge and start writing, these two hit the ground running. The Overachiever was busy telling me that my bar wasn't high enough, and that I needed more pages and insights. Meanwhile, the Superhero egged me on and fueled my enthusiasm. But what happened when I experienced my first bump in the road…? In came the Shadow and his mistrusting attitude. *What if I take on too much? What if I can't finish it in time? What if I make a mistake?* He's all about questioning and creating doubt.

Because I've gained a sense of self-awareness, I was able to stop myself right then and there. I knew the Shadow had stepped in and was trying to protect me. I was able to acknowledge him and thank him for caring. But rather than letting everything spiral into discouragement, I was able to tell my Shadow to stop.

See, the beautiful thing about learning to speak the language of your facets is that you don't ever have to let a power struggle occur. If you understand all of them, you know why they're there. And you can choose to let them help you, rather than hinder your life.

Become a Negotiator

Becoming powerfully present with yourself means learning how to negotiate with your different parts to create harmony, peace, and understanding within yourself. Once you master this, you can then learn to extend it to the people around you. Now take a moment to think about your own facets. Where do they come from? What do they do to help you? How do they hold you back? What are their triggers?

Next, I want you to think of a situation, and take a minute to think of which facets were fighting for power. Who won? If you had more self-awareness, would you have modulated the internal power struggle differently? If so, would the results have been different? In what ways?

By taking the time to become self-aware, you can learn how to use your facets to help you, rather than hinder you. It also gives you the awareness to understand when your different facets are coming out, flexing their muscles, and why. Ultimately, this increased understanding allows you to be in full awareness of your thoughts, feelings, and actions. When you come from this place of power and peace, you no longer look for outside validation, confirmation, or reaffirmation—because you're certain about who you are and why you choose to act the way you do.

This knowledge is freedom and liberation. And who doesn't want that?

Summary of Presence

Learning how to be present with yourself takes time and purposeful action. As you cultivate your skills, you can learn what it means to be fully aware of yourself and comfortable with your facets. So take some time to learn and internalize the steps below:

- **Take time to get to know yourself and your facets.**

  Figure out why each of them is part of you. Learning about your different protectors and cheerleaders will help you recognize them when they surface in any given situation.

- **Pay close attention to the way you're feeling.**

  For those of you who think this part of the book is particularly daunting, this step is a good place for you to start. When you start paying more attention to yourself and how you're feeling, you're better able to decide when and how to respond to situations.

  And you can begin to train yourself to always think before you act. Practicing this self-discipline will allow you to become more in tune with yourself and less controlled by your emotions.

- **Take some time for yourself.**

  When learning to become more self-aware and present, you must be willing to truly listen to yourself. For someone who is just starting this journey of becoming self-aware and present, it's hard to get anywhere when you're constantly being bombarded by hundreds of other distractions and environmental stimuli.

Make it a point to carve out some much-needed you time, so you can communicate with yourself and get in tune with the many ways you're feeling.

- **Be as kind to yourself as you are to others.**

  It's so easy to be overly judgmental of ourselves. Most of us are our own harshest critics. As you're learning to be more present, make sure you're being kind to yourself and forgiving yourself for the problems and flaws in your personality. These are simply opportunity areas for growth.

  If you're kind to yourself and nourish yourself deep down within your soul, you'll be much happier and healthier.

  Being present with yourself and others is a profound and healing part of finding self-love. If you fall in love with the process of learning about your inner depths, you'll be well on your way to mastering self-love.

  It's a beautiful journey.

Selflovology Tips for Presence

- Spend time alone, purposely doing activities you enjoy. That way, you can only be present with yourself.

- When you engage in conversation, really listen, instead of waiting for the person to stop speaking.

- Be intentional in your relationships.

- Be honest and authentic in all your interactions.

- Spend time with your friends and loved ones in silence. Become comfortable with the uncomfortable, and practice being together without doing anything.

- Make an effort to be aware of what is happening now, instead of worrying about what will happen later.

- Find your calling.

Chapter 4

It's Okay Not to Be Okay

> *"If I ever go looking for my heart's desire again, I won't look any further than my own back yard. Because if it isn't there, I never really lost it to begin with!"*
>
> **Dorothy, The Wizard of Oz**

I'm sure you've heard people say that the grass is always greener on the other side. Most people have looked at their own lives and thought, "If only I had this or looked like that, things would be so much better… "

One of the major issues with this ideology is that most of us always want more. If we have the car, the job, and the friends, we think, "If only I was married." But then when we have that, we think, "If only we had a bigger house." As a society, we struggle to feel satisfied, which can leave us feeling unfulfilled. Moreover, we often spend time and energy comparing our lives, situations, mindsets, and life journeys to other people's.

It's totally natural to compare and judge; it's part of being human. We constantly evaluate, make judgements about things and people, and let our perceptions shape our world views. However, there's a basic problem with this way of interacting with the world: We often base our own self-worth on a fraction of the picture we see.

Imagine you see a man wearing a designer suit and crossing the street holding his equally well-dressed daughter's hand. As they approach their glistening BMW, they're smiling. They get in and drive away, and you're left thinking, "Wow, I wish I had a life like his. He looks so happy. He looks like he really has his life figured out. He has nice clothes, so he must be wealthy. He must have a wonderful job, and he and his partner must be happy living a lavish life with their adorable, well-behaved children."

Let me stop there. Do you see the issue I'm eluding to? Oftentimes, the moments we see are often just that: moments in time. We attach feelings, emotions, and perceptions to glimpses of someone else's life, and let them impact how we feel about ourselves and our own lives.

What we don't see is how these people we're comparing ourselves to live day-to-day. If we did, we'd realize we're all the same. We all struggle. Some days, we feel like we're conquering life, and other days, we feel like we're barely keeping it together.

This is all part of the human experience. No one has it all together all the time. Read that again. No one. When you find your mind wandering to this place of toxic comparison, remind yourself that you are seeing a very carefully curated fraction of someone's life. No one puts their hardest moments on display. We haven't learned yet as a society that this is okay.

In this chapter, we'll explore what it means to understand ourselves in the context of the world around us. We'll also examine why no one can—and should—be perfect all the time.

Living a Life You Love

Only after I acknowledged that I wasn't okay, I started learning how to be more than okay. Let me unpack that. Once I gave myself the permission and grace to not always be perfect, I began to see that my true self was good just the way I was. I saw myself with eyes of acceptance and compassion and realized that I was not a sum of my possessions and achievements. I began to see into the core of my being and there I found myself to be more than enough.

This is the essence of self-love.

It is nuanced, yet it is also simple. The core of self-love is finding the goodness which already exists within yourself and living your life from this place of purity and peace. You have everything you need within your very soul. The search must always be inward—deeper, further to your most honest self that is made of pure love.

It's a returning home.

The essence of self-love is a returning to your core being. You can work to become better at quickly accessing this part of yourself. You can become better at drowning out all of the other voices—listening only to the voice of your own soul.

When I began living from this place of self-realization, I moved through the world with much more ease and I began to trust that I was enough.

You are more than enough, too. Even on your worst days, your inner core does not change. You are who you are deep down no matter what is going on around you. You could be having the hardest day of your life, and the truth is even on that day—you are at your deepest core totally and completely enough.

No one and no situation outside of your control will ever change this. It is and always will be the truth. There is a lot of freedom in this knowing. Now you can move about in the world with a deep sense of security. Things on the surface may try to rattle you and question your worth, but nothing can touch that peace within you.

So, yes, it's okay not to be okay because you know the truth. No matter how much chaos is swirling around you, the capacity to re-turn to your peaceful core is always within your control. No one can take this away—ever.

So, what does this mean for your life? Do not allow the fact that you're not okay on the surface stop you from living a life you love. Don't become a victim. Realize and accept the fact that this is just a tiny moment in the grand scheme of your life and you can always return to your core.

Make this a daily practice. Like meditation, you can remove yourself from the onslaught of negative feeling and emotions and tap into the peace within yourself that reminds you that you are perfect just the way you are.

Like meditation, it takes some practice. The world will continue to scream at you trying to steal your peace. Find a way to drown out the noise and tap into your perfect core—the truest place within yourself.

Mantras help focus your mind and drown out the negative voices. Simply repeat a phrase that brings you back. I like to say, "I deeply love and accept myself... "

Over time and with awareness and practice, you will become the victor in your story. Then you'll be well on your way to mastering your self-love.

Now take a breath now and repeat after me: "My world is perfect just the way it is. I will learn and grow through everything life brings me. And through it all, I do not always have to be okay. It's okay to feel my emotions, be present, and even not be okay sometimes. This fluctuation is natural, and it doesn't make me any less worthy."

The truth is we oftentimes look for happiness and validation from things outside ourselves. If we live through someone else's lens, it can be difficult to gauge and balance our own thoughts and emotions, which is a slippery slope. As we gain more validation from external sources, we base our decisions and actions on how others respond to us. As the incongruence of our actions and feelings grows, we get further and further away from ourselves, which leaves us unsure about what to make of the inner turmoil. Outside validation can never soothe our inner emotions and personal thoughts; this can create a vicious cycle that leaves us feeling alone and confused about who we really are.

Here's the thing: Some of your current habits, friends, and hobbies are influenced by expectations outside yourself. As you journey towards self-love, you need to start taking those outside opinions less seriously. While you're reading *Selflovology*, you need to start paying attention to what really matters deep down inside yourself.

By reaching within yourself, you can feel your struggles, and start seeing the beginning of a better you. As you start knowing and loving yourself, you also start seeing that all of your feelings and experiences are wonderful, and don't need to be hidden or validated. You are good just the way you are.

I'm not suggesting that everything you'll feel in your life will feel great in the moment, but with self-love, you'll realize that not every single thing that happens to you contributes to the big picture of who you are. You are perfect despite what happens to you or around you. Your core is solid. You know who you are. And you are good.

Everything you could ever want or need is already inside you. You just have to unleash it by loving yourself enough to be your true self.

So how do you do that? Focus on overcoming obstacles and aggravations with acceptance and grace.

Carefully consider who you want to be and how you may already have what you need within you already. By knowing and loving yourself at your deepest core, can you see how you can take steps towards that vision?

Learn to see opportunity, and if it comes down to it, remind yourself that even the most beautiful lotus flowers grow out of marshlands. Right now, you're not defined by your circumstances, and you haven't ever been defined by them. Remember, life happens *for* you, not *to* you. You are 100% okay—no matter what.

The most powerful piece of advice I can give you is to listen to yourself more often than you listen to others. Everyone in your life has a reason for wanting you to be a certain way, even if they have the best intentions. Now that we've seen how other people's expectations may prevent self-love, we can be okay with that.

Grow in self-awareness, and refrain your mind from falling back into old habits. Create new habits. It's easier than you think and so very worth the effort. Approach situations with this new understanding an awareness of how it makes you feel. No matter how loud your extrinsic motivators are, let your intrinsic motives guide you.

Here's another important lesson to learn: knowing the difference between being positive when overcoming obstacles, and allowing negativity to naturally process within. Being okay with an obstacle doesn't mean that you should pretend. I'm not talking about faking it until you make it. Rather, I'm talking about acknowledging the situation and becoming comfortable knowing that you'll always be okay if you're letting your inner core and inner voice guide you.

Don't let expectation or pressure allow you to deviate from what you know is right for you in your life. Walk confidently on your path, and never settle for something less than what you desire. If you allow an outside force to live your life for you, you'll only end up disappointing yourself. Learn your inner power, and learn to trust that you know what's right for you.

No matter where you came from and how you ended up reading these words, from this moment on, you can choose self-love. I chose betterness, and I want you to make that choice as well. Each of you has that power with yourselves—even as you read these words.

I could only make that choice when I learned that it's okay not to be okay. It's okay to struggle and not be sure where you'll end up. It's okay to feel like you don't fit in with your family, friends, and class-mates. It's also okay to decide that it's time for something different in your life. It may take some time to hear yourself, but if you listen, you'll learn exactly what mastering self-love means to you.

More simply, being okay with not being okay involves learning how to overcome what we think we have to be, being true to ourselves, and moving toward self-love time and time again—no matter what is going on around you.

Trusting you can control your own happiness allows you to process and accept the uncertainty and imperfections in your own life. Some questions to help you process them:

- How do you see yourself?

- More precisely, how do you feel about how you see yourself?

- Can you be who you are and feel okay?

- Does someone in your life make you feel like you're not okay, or that you should be something you're not?

- Do you feel like you have to pretend in certain situations?

- Are the people in your life supportive?

- Are the people you choose to allow into your life okay with you not being okay?

The Beginning of My Journey

When I turned 18 years old, I told my mom point-blank that I was going to look for a therapist. Like many cultures, the culture I come from says that our children are perfect, so they don't need any help. And that's what my family immediately told me.

But I knew I needed to gain a greater understanding about why I thought and acted the way I did, and I felt like I needed clarity and guidance about my cyclic behavior. In my relationships, I always attracted people who needed saving. And in my work, I always limited myself about what I could accomplish.

I knew I needed to work on myself. So I got a referral for a therapist that a friend of mine was seeing, and I figured it was now or never. I knew it would be a relief to finally be able to talk some things out. For years, I tried to uphold the expectation that I was perfect, and there was nothing wrong with me. Then when I walked into the first session, I finally faced reality:

I was simply not okay.

In fact, as soon as I walked in, I didn't even get a single word out. I burst into tears. It was like all my suppressed emotions were flowing out of me faster than I could control. The therapist was so patient and calm. He took one look at me, laughed, and threw me a half-used tissue box. He waited until I was able to stop crying, and said, "This is why you are here."

I knew my time of running from my emotions was over. It was time to do the work and face my pain, once and for all. My therapist had a big bookshelf made of dark wood. He walked past all the rows of books, one by one. Then he stopped and pulled out a book called *Codependent No More: How to Stop Controlling Others and Start Caring for Yourself*. When he handed me that book, I didn't realize the weight it would carry in my life.

After our first session, I felt lighter than I had in years. I drove to the bookstore and picked up the book he recommended. Eagerly, I headed to the checkout, thinking, "I'm about to take a crash course in how to live." And I was right.

As soon as I opened the book, the first story was about a young girl who'd gone through exactly what I'd gone through. She grew up with an alcoholic father and was codependent in her first relationship. It was like I was reading my own story, word for word. For the second time that day, I started crying. I wasn't alone after all.

I'd found what I'd been looking for: hope.

It was so hard for me to keep reading, as page after page perfectly described my life story. But after I read it for a while, I realized that many of the problems I'd tried to fix in others were actually problems within myself. It was like I was waking up for the first time.

Reading that book was the first step in realizing that it's okay not to be okay, which became the beginning of my journey towards self-love.

Save Yourself

By realizing the importance of my self-worth and self-love, I saw that trying to save anyone from their own choices will only end in destruction. From there, I was able to learn for the first time that you can't control anyone else, because it will only end in negativity, hatred, and hurting. You actually end up with bigger problems than the people you're trying to help, because they have their own lives and their own challenges.

As you'll see when we get deeper into the discussion, self-love involves meeting someone where they are and loving yourself, regardless of anyone else's opinion. It also involves acknowledging that no one in a relationship is responsible for another person's happiness or choices.

For me, acknowledging this need for support, guidance, and learning was a kind of release. It allowed me to be upset, and to not be perfect. Then I could learn and grow in a way that would work for me.

When I realized how healthy it is to be open about not being perfect, it was the start of something big. I'm telling you this because I've gone through it, too. For so many years, I didn't seek anything because I chose to let outside influences deter me from doing what I wanted and needed to do. Finally choosing to seek help was my first step in realizing it's okay to not be okay.

Healing only occurs after the wounds are acknowledged. Remember that.

When people see you cry, you're vulnerable to them, but you're also being honest. In the world we live in, the lack of focus on mental health issues is a big, big problem. By opening your minds to your positive and negative feelings, you gain more honesty and a deeper level of self-love. It comes down to loving yourself, even in the bleakest of times.

Composure is a front. It isn't sustainable to healing. It doesn't allow for healing or understanding. It simply allows us to keep our outside image perfect and unscathed, but does that matter when you're lost and hurting inside? See the power in taking ownership of your emotions. It takes courage to face your pain, and it allows for true healing to occur.

When it comes down to it, we must realize our outsides are simply shells. We all know this deep down. When our time here has passed, our bodies will fade away. So it makes no sense at all to spend a majority of time and efforts on our shells. Don't get me wrong, staying healthy and taking care of our bodies is so important, but we do not need to do this for others. This should be done because *we* want to *feel* better. The opinions of others should not color this act of self-love toward our bodies and our physical wellbeing.

Emotional Sludge

For a moment, remove yourself from the picture. If you had a friend or family member who confided in you, would you see them as weak or less than? No? Then I beg the question, why is it that you don't perceive their vulnerability as weak, but you don't extend that kindness to yourself?

Many of us are guilty of being fixers. We love to help others, but never prioritize helping ourselves. We have limitless compassion and understanding for others, but we fail to offer these same gifts of grace to ourselves. It's our turn to retrain our minds to learn to perceive all emotions with a welcoming attitude, and allow them to exist.

We must learn to feel everything, accept and realize those feelings are okay, and move through them. *Through* them. This is the key. We have to go straight through what we are feeling to gain the lessons. If we try to circumnavigate the difficulty of walking through our emotions, we will only find ourselves right back at this same place in the future. The soul will continue to try to teach you until you are truly ready to learn.

For a moment, imagine that you're a river. Allowing emotion to flow through you is like a river with a gentle beautiful current. Things are moving; the water remains clear, and the ecosystem is healthy and well-nourished.

Now imagine that same river, but it's filled with rocks and debris that are obstructing the natural flow of the water. What happens? The water becomes trapped and stagnant. Debris builds up, and the water that was once perfectly clear becomes sludgy and soiled. If you don't let your emotions flow through you, you'll become over-loaded with emotional sludge, too. If you trap unpleasant emotions without acknowledging them, they won't be able to flow. How much emotional sludge are you allowing to exist in your mind?

Now give yourself a moment to feel those emotions. Allow them to flow through your mind, acknowledge them, and let them go. Appearing strong isn't worth carrying the extra baggage. Believe me. Free yourself from the confines of always having to be strong, and learn to be okay with the range and depth of all your emotions. They're natural, and they don't make you less weak or more burdensome. In fact, being in touch with your emotions—knowing them, feeling them, naming them, and allowing them to flow through will make you more self-aware and will increase your compassion and empathy for others and for yourself. Accept all of it as learning—placed in your life for your growth and wellbeing and move forward.

Once you truly realize and accept it's okay not to be okay, you'll be better equipped to walk through the many storms of life. Being okay with not being okay is being accepting, and encouraging people to find their way through it with whatever help they need.

Once you are open to your own opportunities for growth, you will become more open to other people's vulnerabilities. You will now be equipped to spread love or show support, instead of being uncomfortable. Life gets messy, ugly, and cruel, and having to hide that and filter it for our viewing public takes away from our self-mastery. Plus, it just doesn't feel good to deny this very vital aspect of our humanity. We are deeply feeling beings. We must allow this part of ourselves to come out of the shadows and into the light.

If we expect everyone to be at their best and brightest around us, we're not being real. Facing reality involves seeing the struggles in ourselves and others. I've struggled with this concept in many different ways. And over the years, I've found different ways of overcoming my low self-worth by seeking help for myself.

Effective ways of dealing with not being okay are different, depending on what helps you personally or what you're struggling with. While a spa day or meditation might work for some, others find it more therapeutic to work out or keep busy.

Here are some suggestions for turning down days into growth moments:

- Seek a mentor outside your inner circle.

- Practice positivity through simple things like deep breathing.

- Be transparent while sharing your truth.

- Devote time to something that speaks to your heart.

- Listen to motivational music or words.

- Remove fear from the situation.

- Make a list of everything you want to change, and one step you can take to achieve each item now.

- Choose a comforting activity, and let your body recharge.

Summary of Outlook

In my journey, one of the biggest things I discovered is that we can only control our own happiness. I learned not to try to control anybody, and not to expect to be the cause of someone's happiness.

Once you understand you can only control and help yourself, you can let go. As I worked through my own issues, I found I could let go in other areas of my life. And I realized a lot of things in life are completely beyond our control, which is a huge step toward self-love.

How much time do you spend on negative self-talk? It can include:

- The thoughts inside your head the moment you wake up to.

- The verbal complaints you make throughout the day.

- The long list you use to describe how something that happened to you wasn't fair.

Daily, remind yourself that life is happening for you. Remind yourself that you're not defined by your circumstances. Remind yourself to be aware of all of your emotions, thoughts, and actions.

Remember that it's okay to not always be okay.

There's no place like home. It's time to return. You have everything you need. You are enough.

More than enough.

Selflovology Tips for Outlook

- Find a prayer or mantra you can repeat when stress builds up.

- Acknowledge the hard feelings and pain, and understand they make us stronger.

- Ask for help with little things from the people in your life.

- Make a list of all the hurts and past problems, then burn it.

- Choose one negative thing you repeatedly tell yourself, and write out all the reasons why it's not true (or workarounds if it actually is true).

- Look in the mirror, and say something positive about your day.

- Read a book that promotes self-development and love.

- Dig deep into your emotions, and discover where they come from.

- Give yourself permission to get emotional.

Chapter 5

Self-Awareness

> *"What is necessary to change a person is to change his awareness of himself."*
>
> **Abraham Maslow**

Even though most people think they have self-awareness, the reality is that most of us aren't even aware enough to realize that "self-awareness" is nothing more than misplaced self-judgement. I know you're probably thinking that I'm making a harsh claim here, but bear with me and allow me to explain. Self-awareness is such a powerful force that most people are intimidated by the idea of truly understanding their own constant inner banter. In fact, they would rather say they're self-aware than actually feel the weight of true self-awareness.

So, what does it mean to be truly self-aware? In essence, self-awareness involves understanding who you are, and what your strengths and weaknesses are. Sounds simple enough, doesn't it? The challenge becomes understanding and dissecting our truths, so we can understand:

- The habits we keep.

- The choices we make.

- Why we make them.

- Most importantly, coming to a place of self-moderation and cognizant action, rather than a misguided reaction fueled by emotions.

So now that we've defined self-awareness, how can we learn to become more self-aware?

Luckily, increasing our self-awareness can be learned by following these five simple lessons:

Lesson 1: Understand Your Distractions

Life is full of distractions, including work, family, day-to-day chores, traffic, music, and TV shows. If you're not careful, these simple distractions can overtake your life. And we wonder why some of us feel like we lack purpose. By learning what your distractions are, you'll be able to understand what you want to focus your time on.

Some distractions are unavoidable. You cannot simply not show up to work, and you have to deal with traffic to be able to get there. And unless you've mastered the art of photosynthesis, you'll need to visit a grocery store at least once a week.

However, there are ways to manage these distractions that will allow you to have more time to spend on listening to yourself, and coming to an awareness of what you really want in this life. While it may be easier to distract yourself with whatever you're dealing with in your life, these endeavors will never cultivate a sense of self. And let's be perfectly honest: You cannot run from yourself forever.

By increasing your awareness of your distractions, you will naturally become more aware of what you're trying to distract yourself from, whether it be your own insecurity, guilt, or fear. After you eliminate unnecessary distractions, you'll be able to dissect and understand these emotions better. Therefore, they'll no longer be able to rule your conscious mind.

Let me give you an example from my own life. I used to suffer from panic attacks. They would always catch me off-guard, and I focused on fearing their presence, instead of learning my triggers. For a long time, I let my distractions become my coping mechanisms, until I came to the realization that I was airing out my dirty laundry by ignoring (or choosing not to practice) self-awareness. My panic attacks would sneak up on me, because I chose to distract myself, rather than prepare myself and moderate my responses to stress.

I remember the night when I learned that focusing on distractions is not a coping mechanism, but a blatant disservice to my health and wellbeing. I ended up in the hospital, hooked up to a device that was blowing air up my nostrils. There were machines around me. Everything was foreign, and to make things worse, everything was beeping and chiming nonstop. I was covered in cold sweat that made my skin stick to the misshapen mattress on the ER gurney. I couldn't breathe. It was like my heart was about to jump out of my chest. I couldn't move, but I also couldn't sit still.

More about that night later. For now, here's the point: I realized that I'd brought this moment of pure discomfort on myself. By ignoring my thoughts and allowing the distractions to drown out my internal conversation, I'd gotten to the point where my emotions spilled out all at once. So I was ultimately paying the price for my chosen ignorance.

You see, problems don't go away just because we choose to ignore them. We can drown out our inner thoughts for a while, but I promise you, "a while" only lasts so long before the body refuses to hold the weight any longer. Eventually, the body will manifest physical symptoms of emotions left unexpressed. You'll need to listen to yourself, and come to a place where you're no longer fighting to keep the lid on your thoughts and emotions.

Sounds simple, but it takes a lot of unlearning. First, we are not taught to feel our feelings and emotions. Second, we are not taught that our feelings are valid and are of great importance. Third, we are not taught to express our inner thoughts, feelings, and inner dialogue.

We rarely have healthy emotional lives to look toward as we are growing up and establishing our own emotional rhythms. We see hustling and doing. We rarely, if ever, see just simply *being*. We don't see what it looks like to be still within our feelings. This is in large part because the people before us simply did not know how to feel or express. It feels unsafe, risky, and it's just easier to stuff emotions rather than feel them.

What we see and are taught is to get over it. Move on. Let it go. We are taught to deny and ignore our humanity. We are taught to suppress our feelings and hide our emotions. We are taught to put on a happy face and get on with life.

This type of emotional stuffing down and "pull yourself up by your bootstraps" mentality has been passed down from generation to generation for centuries. It is how people have survived for ages. But that's all it is.

Survival. It's not truly living, and it's nowhere near thriving.

For some, the bootstraps eventually break and the emotional dams overflow. And for others, sadly, they live their entire lives never truly knowing their emotional beings.

This is not where I want to be, and if you are reading this book, I know this is not where you want to be either. Hear me when I say you do not have to live the lives of the people before you. You can live in absolute abundance and joy. You can live in complete alignment with your thoughts, beliefs, and feelings. You can live a beautiful life full of purpose and meaning. You can connect with yourself and others in ways you never thought possible.

You can be whole.

And by living wholeheartedly you will be like a beacon of light to others—inspiring them and giving them permission to seek the same richly abundant life for themselves. Like a pebble dropped in still waters, the ripple effects are undeniable.

By embracing and learning self-awareness, you learn to differentiate the everyday things that are real from the ways you distract yourself from what you really feel and think. Now take some time to reflect on the types of habits you have that serve as distractions.

After a long day, do you go have a drink at the bar to help you reset? If so, what emotions are you distracting yourself from? When you and your significant other get in a fight, do you go for a drive and blast music to help calm yourself down? If so, what emotions are you distracting yourself from?

If you choose to deny indulging your distractions and instead sit with your feelings and emotions, you'll come to a place of greater awareness about how you feel, and why you feel that way. With this new understanding, you'll need fewer distractions, because you'll be able to process emotions as they appear, rather than pretending they don't exist.

Lesson 2: Notice Your Feelings

This lesson actually illustrates the easiest way to increase your self-awareness. But for some reason, most people fail to recognize how they actually feel. So they choose to react, rather than feel.

Let's return to the night when I was hospitalized due to my panic attacks. There I was on that gurney, with unfamiliar sounds buzzing in my ears. The nurse walked in, and handed me a little white pill, without looking at me. She murmured something along the lines of: "Take it. It will make you feel better." Then she was gone.

I took a moment and tried to understand how I'd gotten here. It was all a blur. I remembered that I'd gotten angry, and that there was some sort of argument. But I couldn't remember how it ended. All I knew was that I suddenly felt my legs go numb, and I was shaking. There wasn't enough air in the room. My vision sort of went black, and the next thing I knew, I was in the back of an ambulance that was pulling into an emergency room parking lot.

I stared at the little pill for another minute, then popped it into my mouth and swallowed it. Afterward, I laid back on the lumpy gurney and looked at the ceiling.

In that moment, I realized how important it is to pinpoint your feelings. If I hadn't ignored my feelings and focused on all my distractions, they wouldn't have engulfed me like a tsunami that night. If I was honest with myself in that very moment, I could have seen that I felt hurt and misunderstood—not angry. However, rather than understanding, acknowledging, and communicating my actual feelings, what did I do? I became angry because I was hurt, and defensive because I was overwhelmed. And I chose to speak without listening because I didn't feel heard.

Do you see what I'm getting at here? When we haven't done the hard work of self-reflection and awareness many of us frequently react with actions that are completely out of line with how we actually feel. Why? Because we're completely detached from our core being.

We are in survival mode. We are constantly trying to protect ourselves. We live in fight or fight mode. It's a completely natural defense mechanism, but it doesn't allow us to resolve our own inner turmoil. Rather, we confuse how we actually feel with how we express our feelings, which leads to further self-denial.

By becoming more self-aware, you're able to look within yourself before you react to situations. Therefore, you'll understand exactly how you feel, and why. Based on this understanding, you can express your true feelings, rather than produce counterfeit feelings to protect yourself. Not only does this tactic prevent a lot of confusion, it also helps you communicate your needs, so you'll feel more whole. You will feel like you are living from a place of truth. Truth begets more truth. Once you internalize this new way of thinking and living, you will never go back. The truth will be magnetic. You'll crave more and more.

As you become more emotionally healthy and aligned, when faced with a situation that you would normally just react to, you will now stop and feel. You will become emotionally disciplined. You will no longer just react. Instead, you will look within yourself for the reasons why you feel and think the way you do. If you communicate honestly with the world, you'll watch things change—within yourself and within others with whom you are surrounded.

Lesson 3: Recognize What Your Heart Is Saying

We often get ourselves in trouble by trying to process our feelings with our minds. We are all caught up in our heads trying to rationalize and make sense of our feelings. We tell ourselves how to feel with our minds, rather than letting the process be a matter of the heart. Instead, we need to let matters of the heart be handled by the heart, and matters of the mind be handled by the mind.

Oftentimes, we confuse ourselves by trying to convince ourselves out of what we already know is true. If you're no longer in love with someone you're dating, why stay? If you listened to your heart, you'd leave, wouldn't you? The obvious answer is yes. So why do people frequently choose to stay in relationships in which they aren't satisfied? Because they have allowed the mind to meddle in matters of the heart.

The mind will tell you things like this:

- "Starting over is so hard."

- "You will be so sad."

- "What if you never find someone else who loves you?"

- "This person has potential. They can learn if I teach them, so they'll change if I just stick it out longer."

I'm here to tell you to stop all of that thinking from this moment onward. You don't have the right to fly a plane just because you bought a plane ticket. Similarly, your mind has no right to rationalize and manipulate how you feel because it shares the same body as your heart. Let your heart guide you in matters of love, and don't let your mind come in and take over. This defense mechanism is the most destructive one of all. Learn to recognize your feelings without attaching human judgement and rationalizations to it.

There's no need to explain how you feel. You feel the way you feel, and that's that. If you understand that your feelings may hurt someone else, it doesn't make those feelings any less valid. You can manipulate your feelings by letting your mind meddle with them, but you'll never be able to be honest with yourself about what you want if you operate in this way.

By becoming more self-aware, you learn that you don't have to manipulate your feelings to make room for other people's emotions. You're only responsible for yourself, and how *you* feel. Your emotions cannot—and should not—be marginalized to something your mind can process, because the truth is the mind cannot understand emotions the way the heart can. Your mind is not connected to your core being like your beating heart is.

The heart can speak to the mind, but the mind cannot capture your heart and your feelings in the same way. It's like a work of art. A picture is worth a thousand words because hearing about it will never be the same as seeing it for yourself. Learn when to ask your mind for its opinion, and when not to. Do not let yourself get involved in an internal battle between two forces that don't speak the same language. This will only cause confusion, inner chaos, and further disconnection from your true self.

Lesson 4: Find Self-acceptance

Self-awareness can either be a blessing or a curse, depending on which lens you choose to view it through. It allows you to see yourself for everything you truly are. In other words, you don't only see all the wonderful things that make you who you are; you also see your own flaws and the things you need to work on to become a better person.

Increasing self-awareness while wearing the lens of judgement will lead to increased self-doubt, because we're able to see everything. We're no longer hiding behind our minds, distractions, and reactions. We can see the myriad ways that others judge us, so we regress. However, if we learn to become self-aware through the lens of self-acceptance, we will feel more empowered.

What does this look like? This looks like openness with clear and healthy boundaries. It's okay to ponder the opinions of others, however we must become so crystal clear in our own existence that we can take the good and quickly discard the bad. Just because someone has an opinion about us does not make it true. We can refine our filters and only allow in that which will serve to make us better.

Just because we can see and understand who we are and why we are the way we are, we don't necessarily become less worthy of our own love. Self-awareness strips us of everything extraneous, and leaves us vulnerable. If you can find the beauty in that rawness, you'll be able to relish this new self-understanding, and carry it into your day-to-day life. Vulnerability is not weakness. Quite the opposite in fact. Vulnerability is strength and takes courage to live your life from this place. But really, why would anyone want to live any other way?

The vulnerable and honest life is the best life. Because it is the truth. Once we learn to be vulnerable with our own selves—allowing ourselves to feel without judgement—we can offer this gift of grace to the people around us.

Self-awareness and self-judgement cannot coexist.

Imagine a photograph of a woman posing nude in front of a mirror. The photo is beautiful, artistic, and classy, and it speaks volumes in a single shot. People could stare at the photo for hours, and discuss the significance of it.

This is awareness.

People are simply appreciating the photos for the beauty and simplicity it reveals. They notice the shadows and the light, the mixture of emotions on the woman's face. They see her humanity and honor it. They notice the soft curves of her body and imagine all that she has done in her life—given birth to babies, taken care of others... There is no judgement. Just awareness and appreciation.

Now imagine people looking at the same exact photo and narrowing in on negativity. Someone immediately notices a small amount of cellulite on the woman's upper thigh. Then someone points out the folds of skin on her belly, and notices how imperfect her hair is. They are only seeing the flaws. They are completely and utterly missing the point. They are not seeing the woman's body as a beautiful vessel that has brought forth life. They are simply choosing to see the imperfections.

This is judgement.

Which person do you want to be? If you were the woman in the photograph which person would you want taking in your reflection. This is an easy answer. No one wants to be judged. We should strive to learn to be the aware person rather than the judgmental person. It's a simple shift. And it's a daily choice. It can, and will be, life-altering for you as you are on your own journey toward self-love.

By practicing the extension of this grace to others, we will start to slowly extend this same measure of grace to ourselves. We will start to simply become aware of ourselves without any judgement. We will see our own reflection and we will appreciate the lines on our faces—for we have lived and laughed—the lines are a beautiful reminder of where we have been. We will observe and thank our bodies for carrying us all of these years. We will see its strength and in it we will see no flaws. The imperfection we see will become perfect—the truest reflection of our life and our humanity.

Imagine this level of radical self-acceptance and self-love. My heart races at the possibility of what our lives could become—what our world could become—if we all lived from this place.

Just imagine...

Summary of Self-Awareness

Learn to be reflective with purpose. Becoming self-aware doesn't need to lead you into an emotional crisis because you realize all the things that make you flawed. It seeks to show us who we are at our core, so we can learn to correct or discard the things that don't serve us. Self-awareness isn't a crisis; it's a gift. Your flaws don't have to decrease your own intrinsic value—in fact they can become your strongest attributes. Through self-acceptance and self-awareness, you grow these parts of yourself—refining them over time. You will live in a place of hope and light. This is self-love.

Self-awareness is a lesson of the heart, and you need to practice it daily in order to get better at it. It is the most important work you will ever do. Take it slow. Be kind to yourself during this learning process. It's not going to happen overnight. Be patient. Acknowledge the changes you see and feel happening within yourself as it will spur you on and lead you to keep walking this path. You will slowly come home to your truest and most honest self. You will acknowledge and celebrate yourself for *all* that you are (and aren't), without a single ounce of judgement.

What freedom... What joy...

To be a lover of your own soul, your own best friend, and your own biggest cheerleader... To *really* see and love yourself unconditionally. Can you even imagine how this would radically change your whole entire life?

It's revolutionary.

What are you waiting for?

Selflovology Tips for Self-Awareness

- Pay attention to what is distracting you, and why.

- List three things that trigger you. How can you overcome each of them?

- Be aware of your feelings—not just what you feel, but why?

- Every day, answer this question: Are your actions in alignment with how you feel?

- Be intentional about how you respond to your feelings. Feel before you react.

- Listen to your heart, instead of rationalizing what isn't true. Nourish your self-acceptance.

Chapter 6

Finding Faith

> *"Now faith is confidence in what we hope for and
> assurance about what we do not see."*
>
> **Hebrews 11:1NIV**

Before we go any further, I want to take a second to stop and tell you that faith—as it unfolded in my life—has been one of my most important milestones. By the end of this chapter, you will be clear about the power of perseverance and determination, and you will be equipped and empowered with the tools to make your future goals little everyday reminders, so you'll never stray too far from where you're going. Okay, let's delve right in.

First, I want you to think about how you define faith. Everyone has a different definition of faith, right? For some people, faith is closely tied to a religious institution. For others, faith is trusting in the here and now—being at peace with the plan this life has for them. For others still, faith is praising the earth and being present in each moment, grateful to be able to exist in this universe.

There is no right or wrong way to have faith, but the truth is that we all have some sort of it. We are all spiritual beings whether we recognize it within ourselves or not. We all put our faith in something, someone...

As far as divine purpose, faith goes beyond belief; it extends into our faith in people and circumstances as well. I'm sure we can all think of at least one person or event that has sharpened our faith, inspired us, or given us hope. Furthermore, the concept of faith seeps into our belief in the good of people and that all circumstances in our life are working together toward our good. Oftentimes, you hear people say, "That person gives me faith in humanity." Or conversely, "That person could make me lose faith in humanity."

Here's my point: The term *faith* has a broader definition than we may generally think. In and of itself, faith is neither simply a religion nor a belief system. Faith is deeply personal—unique to each person and quite nuanced. Faith is the path to find peace. It is the intersection between our moral compass and the lens through which we see the world. My definition of faith may be very different than yours, and that's okay. But for all of us, faith gives us hope, peace, and the strength to continue on—despite adversity.

Faith gives us the power to believe in the things of this world that are intangible and unseen—love, kindness, mercy, compassion... This list could go on and on. In our humanity, we see so very little. We see the tip of the iceberg when the reality is it delves endlessly below the surface. There is so much that we are unable to comprehend. If we were able to see the whole of our lives—every single step—we would be utterly consumed. We don't have the capacity to process this vastness.

So, we have faith. We trust that though we cannot see the whole staircase, the next step will be revealed to us when the time is right to move forward. We have faith in people. We look for the good in everyone. We trust the power of love and see the impact kindness has on the world around us. Faith allows us to have compassion for others that we do not know or understand because deep down we trust that they would do the same for us.

Faith is a beautiful and magical part of our humanity. Faith shines a light on the interconnectedness we share with everyone else living life beside us and our connection with the universe and its rhythms. Faith is an equalizer—a reminder that none of us really know what we are doing. We are all just trusting day after day—putting one foot in front of the other and moving forward in faith.

Faith inspires us to keep hoping as we understand that we may not see the whole picture of our lives yet—and perhaps we never will. When we have faith, seeing just what we need in the moment is enough. Faith and trust brings peace.

I want to take a minute to pause here, and let you think about your faith. Where does it stem from? At what age did you identify what you believed in? Or are you still confused about what your faith looks like? Where do you place your faith? In what things or people do you trust?

Regardless of where you stand, just know that the official definition of faith is quite simple...

> *Faith: complete trust or confidence in someone or something*
>
> **Merriam-Webster**

Your faith doesn't need to have a name, and it doesn't need to have an explanation. It doesn't even need to be defined. But it does need a purpose. As humans, we need faith—in some shape or form—to be able to persevere through the twists and turns of this crazy thing we call life. Without it, we become lost, purposeless, helpless, and hopeless.

The truth is whether we recognize it or not, we all place our faith in something or someone. Some may put their faith in success, in finances, and security. Some put their faith in comfort. If I have x, y, and z then I will be happy—I will be complete.

We all experience faith. What may be different for each of us is whether our faith lifts us up and compels us or whether our faith (and where we place it) weighs and brings us down.

It's an important conversation and an important point of self-reflection that is necessary to the journey of self-acceptance and self-love. It is a deeper layer of our being that we must explore to uncover our core values and beliefs.

Have you struggled with your faith because of things that have happened to you, or things you've endured that you can't make sense of? If so, I hope the next two stories I'm going to tell you will help you define your faith, and allow you to find confidence and hope.

When the Shoe Fits

After my father left, I struggled to define faith in my own life for many years. I wasn't able to have faith in anything because I didn't know what I should believe in. I remember feeling so alienated when people spoke about their faith. I'd listen and silently wonder if I'd ever find the clarity to speak about what I believed in. I clearly recall asking my friends what they believed in, and going to different churches to see if I could find my faith. I read countless books about faith, watched videos on it, and spent hours thinking about what I believed in.

I tried to make it tidy and slap a label on it that said: "This is my faith." And for years, I was not at peace—I was restless and uncomfortable. I felt like I was missing something, and I was so desperate to figure out what it was. At the same time, I was so embarrassed about my indecisiveness about the meaning of faith that I just wanted to give up. But then I realized that if I gave up, I could end up with nothing. Isn't blindly believing in something better than losing hope and purpose?

Here's the problem I kept running into, time and time again: I felt I was borrowing someone else's faith. It felt a lot like borrowing someone else's shoes. They fit well enough, but they just never felt like mine. Now, you may be thinking that I'm crazy for comparing faith to shoes, but hear me out. Are you unsure or confused about your faith? Has it been tested so much that you're not sure if you can still have faith in what you thought you believed? If so, this story is for you.

I was 18 years old, and I was in a mental crisis: I wasn't able to fully decide what I believed in. Then I met this woman who changed my life. To this day, I don't think she knows the impact she had on me, which has made her impact even more massive.

On an overcast Tuesday morning, I walked into my favorite coffee shop and smelled fresh bread and java. I tucked myself into my usual corner booth by the window at the front of the cafe, and I started working. I had my headphones in, so I could listen to music softly while I enjoyed my morning tea. There were a few other familiar faces in the coffee shop—the regulars with their newspapers and briefcases stopping in for quick bites before rushing off to their next appointments.

I loved this coffee shop, because it felt like life just paused when you were inside its light-purple walls. I'd watch people pop in from all walks of life. Some were in a hurry, and others were just living on their own time. I don't know why, but for some reason, this coffee shop just had something special about it. No matter who walked through the doors, we were momentarily all in slow motion, just enjoying the little velvet booths and breathing in the scent of the fresh muffins and bagels. It was as if time didn't exist there. The only thing that mattered was the people. It was a tiny slice of heaven on earth. A place—a respite—of complete contentment.

The owner—a charming older woman—would greet each person like family. And in those moments, life just fell away. Phones were silenced, voices were sweet and kind, and no one was in a hurry (if even for just a few minutes). It was like magic, so in times of uncertainty, it gave me the momentary peace I needed.

That Tuesday morning started like many others. The businesspeople came and went. The college students came with their overloaded backpacks and tired eyes, and made themselves at home at the rickety antique tables that lined the back of the cafe. I was enjoying the peace and quiet. As the morning went on, the sun peeked through the clouds. Then as the afternoon shadows got longer, my teacup emptied. So, I decided to gather my things and leave.

That's when I noticed a woman sitting at a small table across from me. She had her back against the wall; she was knitting and reading a book in a language I couldn't make out. She looked up at me, and we made eye contact. I smiled and complimented her on her knitting.

I'm still not sure what she must have sensed about me. Was it the way I smiled? Regardless, she quickly began asking me questions about my life. It's as if she could sense I was unsettled. That afternoon, I learned my first lesson about finding faith. She told me that faith was like a pair of old shoes. I remember that sentence so clearly. She beamed at me as she said it in her thick European accent: "Faith is like a pair of old shoes."

"Have you ever borrowed a pair of shoes from a friend?" She asked me. "Sure," I replied, not sure how any of this made sense. "Well, you know how it goes. Your friend may wear the same size as you, so your feet fit into them well. And you can walk in them just fine. Right?"

"Right," I replied, still dumbfounded at how we'd gotten on the topic of shoes.

"But when you're wearing those shoes, you can tell they aren't yours," she said definitively. "Your friend may have a different arch than you. Maybe they walk on the inside of their feet more than you. Yes, the shoes fit, but you can tell they aren't yours." She stopped as I nodded my head.

"Well, faith is just like that. You can't wear someone else's faith and expect it to feel like your own. Can you make it fit? Sure, but will it be your own faith? No." I smiled as warmth came across my face.

She went on: "Now imagine putting on your favorite pair of old worn-in shoes. No one else can wear them because they're molded to your feet. They're your favorites because they've been with you through so much, and you've always counted on them because they're the only pair you can wear that don't hurt your feet. With them, you don't get blisters. And they have high-quality soles, so you know your feet won't get wet if you step in a puddle. They're your go-to shoes.

Your faith should feel like these shoes. You don't need to borrow someone's new, shiny shoes. Let's face it: Your own shoes will always feel better on your feet. And you don't have to worry about ruining them—because they're old, worn, and yours. That's how your faith should be.

You grow into your faith. You make it your own, and you feel good in it because it's yours. You believe in it wholeheartedly because it's been with you through everything. Your faith doesn't hurt you or give you blisters. Rather, it gives you hope when times are hard. You can't expect to find faith in everything else. Listen to yourself; you already know what you believe in."

Next, she asked me the question that's remained with me all this time: "So what do you believe in?"

"Love," I responded.

She smiled at me again. "See, you're not having a crisis of faith. You just didn't know what to call it. Your faith is love."

The rest of the conversation is a blur. I don't remember anything after that sentence: "Your faith is love." I felt like I finally had my answer. My faith finally had an identity, and I felt at peace. As she left the coffee shop, I walked to my car. We waved at each other one last time as she climbed into her old Volvo and drove away.

This experience was the beginning of finding my faith, and it's translated into everything that I now do in my life—professionally and personally.

My faith is love.

I help people find their love and through that process they find their peace and their purpose. By defining my faith, I was also able to find the beginning of what would later become my purpose.

You see, faith does not have to be this overly theological endeavor. It can be as simple as love. It is your driving force—the thing that compels you to get up every morning and continue onward. Faith is our hope. Without it life feels too heavy to bear. We must place our trust somewhere in order to live a healthy and meaningful life.

If you still find yourself wondering about your faith, think back to my experience with the woman in the coffee shop. Imagine you are me, and she has just asked you, "so what do you believe in?" Imagine she's sitting across from you smiling—allowing you to absorb and process this question. Then simply respond with what your heart is saying.

This is your truth. This is your faith.

Sometimes, life is funny. It has a way of circling back on itself until you've learned what you need to learn. And while I still had a lot of life to go through to find my purpose, that day was the first time I felt peace that I had faith in something I call love. I hope by sharing this life-altering experience you are able to find that peace as well. Don't give up. It's already within you. Keep searching. You'll know when you find it.

The Gold Dot

The next story I want to share with you is an experience I had when I was 19. It refined my faith and taught me the power of perseverance. With enough determination, I realized I could turn my dreams into reality. In order to reach your goals, you have to be crazy: Crazy passionate, crazy determined, crazy motivated. Your dreams don't just come true by chance. They come true when faith meets passion and drive.

One morning, I received an invite to a convention in Dallas. I eagerly read the invitation, and my excitement grew with each line I read. It was a health and wellness convention, and the keynote speaker was none other than Vince Poscente. I couldn't believe it.

Not only was he a seven-time *New York Times* bestselling author, he was also a role model of mine. I'd watched his YouTube videos and read several of his books. And now I had the chance to listen to him speak in person. I was beside myself with excitement. One month later, I boarded a plane in Los Angeles and made my way to the convention center.

When I walked in, the room was buzzing with the sound of hundreds of excited people eagerly awaiting the day's events. Numerous speakers took the stage, offering words of inspiration and encouragement. With each speaker, the room vibrated with more and more positive energy. You could feel spirits being lifted as the crowd listened to story after story of passion and drive.

Finally, it was time for Vince to take the stage. It was the moment I'd been waiting for. I left my seat and walked to the front of the room so I could be as close to the stage as possible. I didn't want to miss a single word.

And there he was. He walked onto the stage, and the crowd roared. He shared his story about being a professional downhill/speed ski-er. He spoke about the importance of determination and persever-ance, about setting your goals high, and about keeping your aspira-tions higher. I soaked in every single word.

When I left that convention, I was dripping with passion. As I made my way back to the airport, I repeated Vince's advice over and over to myself. I felt ready to conquer the world.

At this point, most people would think the story ends. I went to a convention and learned how important it is to use your faith to per-severe—no matter what it'd require to go from where you are to where you want to be—but it was just the beginning.

The Venue

A few days after I got home, I got a call from Dallas. It was Vince! Keep in mind that thousands of people attended that convention and he walked off to a standing ovation. I was so excited that I felt like a fourteen-year-old girl who'd gotten a phone call from Justin Bieber. But I tried my best to remain calm and said, "How can I help you?"

Apparently, he was looking for a millennial living in Los Angeles. His son was in a band that was going to be performing at the Viper Room on Sunset Boulevard. Since the band was still relatively new, he was trying to get people my age to attend the concert. He didn't want his son to play to an empty room. He asked me if I'd go to the concert, and invite a few of my friends to go with me. In return, he offered to donate his time and speak to my team. I immediately agreed to the offer, and he thanked me and ended the call.

I leapt into action. I knew I couldn't afford to hire him, so this was a big opportunity for me.

By Friday night, all my friends were lined up outside the door of the club to see the concert. Even though he'd only asked me to invite "a few" of my friends to the concert, I brought nearly 50.

So this man (who'd written a book I loved and spoken at a convention that changed my life) emerged from this famous venue, introduced himself to me, looked at the line of people in disbelief, and said, "These cannot all be your friends." When I confirmed that they were, Vince asked, "How did you get them all to be here?" I told him that most of them didn't even know why they were there. I'd just called all of them and told them that if they considered me a friend, they had to show up there on Friday night.

Around 11:30, the security guard approached my friend at the front of the line about entering the venue, and discovered that he was only 18. He told my friend that he had to be over 21 to get in because there was a bar in the venue. So none of us could get in. Knowing there was nothing to be done, Vince told me to send my friends home, and that he'd come speak to my team tomorrow anyway.

But I replied, "I'm just going to figure something out first. Why don't you go in and watch your son start the concert? Just keep your phone on."

I asked my friends not to leave yet. I opened Yelp, and started calling other nightclubs, yoga and pilates studios, and any other nearby spaces I could think of. I relayed the story to each person I called, and told them we needed someone to host us in a nearby space. Of course, as soon as I said that I needed the space for later that night, they all basically said the same thing: "You realize you're talking about 1 o'clock in the morning, and it's Friday night, right?" Then all of them hung up.

Finally, I talked to this guy named Marty. He said, "I feel bad for you, and I totally understand what's going on." But then he said he couldn't do it, like everyone else had. I almost thanked him and gave up, but I stopped and thought for a moment. "What if I paid you $5 per person. Would that work?"

He agreed, so I made arrangements for everyone to meet at Marty's comedy club. When we got there, we discovered there were a few comedians practicing there before performing at the Laugh Factory. So they did stand-up comedy for us while we were waiting, which was great. Then at about 1 a.m., the band came in and played this amazing acoustic performance.

The Gold Dots

While the band was playing, Vince pulled me aside. He told me how amazed he was by what I'd done, and that he'd never forget it, even after traveling all over the world.

When he asked me why I was being so proactive, I told him about almost drinking the beer when I was 12. Then I added, "I thought my decision was going to be the answer to getting over the pain I felt when my dad left, but it wasn't. So I told myself that I was going to choose betterness for the rest of my life, despite the pain, adversity, and challenges I faced."

Right then, Vince looked at me and said, "I want you to close your eyes." Then he put a piece of paper in my hand. He told me to look at it, and I saw a sheet full of gold-dot stickers. Next, he asked me to close my eyes again, and told me to describe myself in the future. "Where do you want to be in the future, even if you have no idea how you'll get there?" So I closed my eyes, took a breath, and told him about the image that clearly appeared in my mind.

"I'm 28 years old, and I just bought my mom her dream home in Malibu. After I walk into the house, I see my dad. He's alive and sober, and he's in the best health and peace of mind he's ever had in his life. I give him a hug and thank him for the decisions he's made in his life, since I wouldn't be who I am today without them.

Then I see about fifty of my family members: uncles, aunts, and cousins. They're filled with the excitement of the moment. Although I'm the first member of my family (in recent memory) to drop out of college to pursue a different life, my purpose in life is clear. As a result, they're proud of me and happy for me.

My mom and I walk out on the balcony overlooking the ocean. I can smell the saltwater, and it's a little windy. As we're standing there, I talk about how I'm thankful for the beautiful life we've been given, and for stubbornly choosing to believe in myself. I hug her and say, "Mama, I did it."

I open my eyes, suddenly aware of the tears that are rolling down my cheeks. I quickly wipe them away as I look from the gold dots in my hands to Vince.

"Good," Vince says, "Now you know why you're so proactive. From now on, these gold dots are going to be your guideposts. Place them everywhere—on your water bottle, on your steering wheel, on your computer, on your TV, and anywhere else where you will see them daily.

Look at them every day. Let them become part of your conscious and subconscious mind. Every time you see them, you'll remember what you're working toward and why. Life has a way of throwing us curve balls time and time again, but use these dots, so you'll never lose sight of your goals, and you'll never stop focusing on what's important.

Have faith that you are in control of your destiny. You are in charge of what happens to you. You just need to believe and work hard every single day to achieve your dreams."

Summary

From that day on, I knew what my "why" was: It was my mom. My faith was in love. I felt clear.

What is your "why?"

What is it that you believe you are on this planet to do? What is your purpose? Why do you exist? These are all huge questions, but when you really take the time to think about them, most people's answers will be quite simple—love, compassion, justice, empathy, joy... When you truly take the time to examine your heart's desire and purpose, the distractions of life—money, fame, success, material possessions—fall away.

These trivial matters no longer matter. They are light and momentary. We realize they can be snatched away at any time. We recognize what truly matters to us. We understand we are on this planet not just to live for ourselves, but we are here to make an impact—to offer our gifts and make the world a better place. The truest essence of our beings rise to the surface when the trivial falls away.

Once you have determined your "why," you will see it is motivated by your faith. They are so interwoven that you can barely untangle them. They can only exist and make the greatest impact when they are peacefully working together through you. Separately they have no meaning and purpose. Together they are magnetic. They are magic.

Who doesn't want that kind of synergy in their life?

Take a moment now, and close your eyes. Then do what I did with Vince that night. I want you to think about and say your "why" out loud. I want you to add as much detail as you can. Think about how that place feels, what it looks like, and what it sounds like. I want you to make it so clear that you could almost touch it if you reached out in front of you. Once you're done, I want you to write your why down on a sheet of paper. I want you to think about it each and every day.

You can even get your own sheet of gold dots and place them strategically around your path. Let the dots be reminders of your "why." The dots can become like breadcrumbs along your path reminding you to keep going and that you are exactly where you need to be to reach your goals. You just need to keep going—day after day—even when life feels heavy and hard.

Have faith. Trust the process. You are becoming.

Selflovology Tips for Faith

- Use your faith to guide you, and let your why lead you on your path.

- Find peace that your goals are within your reach if you choose to be crazy: Crazy passionate, crazy determined, and crazy unstoppable.

- Put on your most comfortable shoes of faith, and entirely believe in your why. You know what you want, so now you can go forward and achieve it. And when life comes in and tries to push you around, use your faith, your gold dots, and your why to create a compass that will keep you moving in the right direction.

Chapter 7

Self-Love Is Your First Love

"So many years of education, yet nobody ever taught us how to love ourselves, and why it's so important."

Unknown

Once you understand that there's a process to finding self-love, you'll start changing the way you live your life day to day. Every day, you will begin to choose better for yourself. Every day you will become stronger. You will refine your faith and grow your trust in yourself—and the people and circumstances that surround you. From this new-found place of peace, you will show the world your strength of character. Every day, you will choose to invest your energy wisely. Every day, you will continue to have the chance to improve yourself, and be better to those around you. Everything related to self-love takes practice, including self-growth and self-awareness.

When you have truly committed yourself to this process of self-love, everything will begin to come into focus. You will have clarity that you never had before. Your vision for your future will be sharpened and your path and purpose will become clearer than ever before.

As you go deeper into this process your relationship with yourself will improve in ways you never thought possible. Your levels of self-awareness and self-acceptance will bring you back to loving yourself—all of yourself. You will see yourself with eyes of grace and compassion. You will look in the mirror and like who you see.

I am smiling ear to ear as I type this for the possibilities this holds for you. It is exhilarating to imagine you, reader, loving yourself unconditionally. Both loving and liking yourself for exactly who you are is life-changing. Keep meeting yourself in the mirror. If you don't yet like and love who you see, keep going. Don't give up. Your breakthrough is just around the corner.

If you don't love yourself, nothing else matters. Period.

It doesn't matter what your intentions are. If you are not operating out of a place of self-love, it is like denying a crucial part of your being. It would be like operating with only the use of one side of your body. Just imagine how lopsided this would feel. You would constantly struggle just to stay balanced—focusing more on not falling over than the task at hand.

This instability will persist until you come into alignment and the only way to do so is through doing the hard work and learning to deeply love and accept yourself.

You can't truly love your spouse and your children if you don't love yourself first. You cannot model a healthy emotional life to your children if you are loathing yourself in private. Kids see through this thin veil. They sense when something is "off." What all kids really want from their parents is their presence. Your spouse and children need you to be fully and completely present. They want the fully aligned you—not the lopsided you.

And this is what you want for them, right? You want them to grow into young adults and adults who love themselves, too. You want them to live wholeheartedly from a place of great love and abundance. So, you have to take your desires for them and believe you are worthy enough to have this for yourself. You must walk your talk.

So regularly reviewing your choices and values are ways to really find ways to love yourself, be yourself, and accept yourself. Ask yourself daily: Am I doing the work? Am I looking for the best within myself? Am I modeling a healthy relationship with self to my family and those whom I love? Am I getting better every day?

Make a daily commitment to the first love of your life: your self-love.

A Difficult Journey

As you've noticed from my stories thus far, the journey to self-love won't be all sunshine and rainbows. To accomplish true love within yourself, the practice can be difficult. Countless struggles have left me wondering if I was doing the right thing, the wrong thing, or anything at all. Finding self-love is not a neat and tidy task. It does not have a clear road map that leads to an X, and there's no welcome committee when you arrive. It requires a vast amount of self-discipline and resolve. No one will be cheering you on—you have to be your own cheerleader. It's a constant journey of growth and self-trust. It is hard work. If it were easy, you would have done it long ago.

Along the way, one of the most powerful things I've learned is to appreciate other people's influence in my life: good and bad. This acceptance—gratitude for all that you have been through as stepping stones—will help you to keep moving forward.

If you recall from the previous chapter, we're not defined by our circumstances but they do shape us. When finding self-love, it's important to become self-aware and grow in gratitude for every moment that has helped you become who you are. Some call it your story or a journey; others just call it life. Whatever you call it, don't let it steal your momentum and your peace. Even if the path has been hard, recognize and give thanks, for this will make you stronger. Wiser. More able to help others who may be going through difficult times in their own life. Struggles can become blessings if we shift our perspective.

Sometimes, life is hard, and other times, it simply doesn't make sense. But over the course of my journey, I've found that every piece of my life has been important. Some experiences have made me wiser, and others have tested my character. But every experience has defined who I am as a human being. While you may be the sum total of your experience, you're not a victim of circumstance. Rather, you're a beautiful culmination of the forces that have allowed you to become the unique individual you are today.

Of course, it's much easier to become angry or resentful about the experiences we feel are unfair and tragic, but that isn't self-love. Let's take a moment to reflect back on all the life lessons I've shared with you thus far. Time and time again, I was faced with situations and challenges, and I could have easily thrown up my hands and given up. But did I? No, because I've found my self-love through those experiences. I wouldn't be writing this book if I'd grown up in a perfectly functional family, or if I didn't choose girlfriends I needed to save. I wouldn't be here if I didn't get bullied. Yes, circumstances challenged me, but a lump of coal doesn't turn into a diamond without adding some pressure, right? (I'm in no way condoning violence or bullying. I'm saying that we can choose how much we let the challenges life presents us with influence us.)

The point is that the life we're living isn't meant to be perfect. It's meant to be perfectly imperfect. And while you may not be able to control everything, you can learn to control your mind, your thoughts, and your actions. And in the end, that's what self-love is all about.

The Importance of Forgiveness

A huge component of self-love is forgiving people, and not being angry about the circumstances that have challenged you throughout your life. Forgiveness is everything. It's easy to hold onto anger, frustration, and distrust, especially when the people we love the most hurt us. Eventually, I was able to let go of those feelings, because I realized forgiveness is mainly for myself.

I used to think forgiveness meant you were saying that you were okay with being mistreated. But since I learned that it's okay not to be okay, I can forgive the pain others have caused me without accepting their behavior.

Holding grudges has long-term implications and stirs up self-hatred that can lead to depression, blame, and isolation. When you hold onto pain that others have caused you, (whether it's due to a death, a divorce, a breakup, abuse, or bullying), you're only causing pain within yourself.

Remember, it's not about getting back at anybody. The only person it's affecting is you. Stop hating others, and start loving yourself. And remind yourself every day that you only go to bed with your own thoughts. Don't let others steal your peace. It's a waste of your energy, and doesn't change the outcome. Invest your energy in smarter ways. Be kind, live without expectations, and let go of the things you cannot control. It will bring you greater peace than anger ever could.

So, if we can forgive the people we want to include in our lives, we can have an ongoing, quiet calmness in our overall lives. Isn't that what self-love really is? It's an overall calmness that allows the anger and vengeance to subside. When we are focused on loving ourselves, we will no longer allow these feelings of unforgiveness to live within us. We've done too much work to go backward. We will quickly find ways to resolve these feelings as not to disrupt the peace and contentment we are growing within ourselves.

We will become strong protectors of our souls. We will only allow good to reside within us. When negative feelings and emotions arise—and they will—our self-love will guide us toward ways to integrate the good lessons these experiences offer and to throw out which is not life-giving.

At first, this process will take some active thought and awareness. You may have to talk it out within yourself to get to the place of letting go. But, with practice and commitment, this process will begin to unfold so seamlessly that you won't even know it's happening. You will naturally take the good and discard the bad and move right along. It will become like a well-oiled machine. I promise.

Responding with Self-Love

Frequently, the most powerful part of self-love is also the most difficult to master: If you learn to accept that other people's responses to you are based on their love of themselves, it opens you up to choosing the interactions you want to have. In other words, if you accept people for who they are and where they are without feeling like you need to change them, you're freeing yourself from unnecessary emotional sludge.

Often, we choose to label people based on their faults, as if they were written in stone. I challenge you to focus on yourself and your reactions to others, rather than attaching labels to people's actions. Be kind. Oftentimes, we only know a fraction of what's motivating people to act the way they do. If the human race could learn more compassion and understanding, we'd foster much healthier, more honest relationships.

However, cultivating that understanding isn't always easy. Oftentimes, it's easy to respond to people rashly. So learn to find your inner peace and calmly respond, rather than mirroring them. It will lead to much greater peace of mind, and allow you to develop an unbreakable sense of self.

The moment you realize how hard others have it, you'll be able to more easily handle the choices they make. On your journey to self-love, it's so important to understand and accept them for who and where they are. Empathy. The power of empathy is boundless. Becoming an empathetic being allows you to sit in another person's experience with zero judgement. You can learn to just simply exist with them in their pain. This is such a gift.

For the most part, we try to understand people, but we usually want to fix them and get back to a comfortable place. Empathy changes everything. We no longer feel the need to fix people and we are willing to feel the discomfort of their pain. We simply accept the experience, and we bear witness to what they are walking through.

Once people know better, they can do better, and some people have to see it through as part of their journeys. Remember, we're only in control of ourselves, so we can't speed up anyone's journey, just like we can't speed up or slow down time. The biggest gift you can offer is a listening ear—and empathetic ear. We know people are already beating themselves up so we must be the voice of kindness that reminds them that they are perfect and loved just the way they are. Radical kindness. Radical empathy. Life-changing. World-changing.

And the first person it will change... is you.

On the journey to self-love, one of the first realizations is that while you can't choose what other people do, you can choose how you react to what they do. You choose how you allow them to make you feel. When you encounter someone full of negativity, you have the ability to absorb or reject that energy.

The choice is wholeheartedly yours. When you love yourself, you know it's not about you. Then, as much as you want to retaliate and push back at the instigator because you feel angry, the truth always reveals itself. So use these moments to further cultivate your self-love.

When you love yourself, you are bulletproof. That is not to say that you don't feel things. You absolutely do. You are more aware of your feelings than ever. The difference is in how you react. You can now respond from a place of love, even if someone is gossiping about you or trying to hurt you. These bullets will now ricochet off of you. You will be able to see them for what they truly are and deny their entrance into your being. You will have clarity. You will see that when these moments occur in life, they're meant to teach you something. You will naturally begin to choose the high road, and rise above the damage they're trying to cause you.

You know better. And you're doing better.

Summary of First Love

The bottom line is that mastering self-love requires you to look within, understand your surroundings, and make choices about how you interact with the world around you.

Now take a moment to reflect on your experiences. Which ones were positive? Which ones were negative? How could you have handled things differently if you knew then what you know now? Are you proud of how you handled yourself?

If you answered no to any of these questions, don't beat yourself up. Now you know better, so now you can do better. We cannot change the past; we can only learn and be more aware in the future. Allow yourself to learn lessons from your experiences, and let the rest go. There is simply no use holding onto anything from your past that stole your happiness or challenged your peace.

Selflovology Tips for First Love

- Every morning, set an intention to do something small and uplifting that cultivates self-love as part of your routine. For instance:

    - Meditate or pray.

    - Read something inspirational.

    - Do an exercise in personal development.

    - Practice yoga or work out.

- For validation, look inside yourself, not the outside world.

- Make a list of everything that makes you excited.

- Focus your life on your passion and purpose, even if you're not certain how you'll accomplish it.

- Find something good about every situation.

- Tell yourself that you can't attract better if you're not willing to be better.

- Remember, your self-love is both your first love and last love.

Chapter 8

Pain as Growth

"Rock bottom became the solid foundation on which I rebuilt my life."

J. K. Rowling

No one enjoys the heartache of a breakup, the sadness of losing a loved one, or the hurt of fighting with someone you really love. The fact is that no one enjoys the negative emotions we all experience, but they are equally important as the positive ones in our lives.

The truth is that pain gives our happiness meaning, as it's a necessary and powerful part of our lives. Everyone experiences difficult, trying, and even devastating times. We can choose to be bitter and carry the pain around, or to put that weight down and rebuild.

Use the things that come into your life as your testimony. Don't be a victim of your circumstances or your past. Instead, celebrate your hard times, for they've led you to learning more about yourself and your strength, and defining your friendships and your boundaries.

Really think about it. Think about the struggles and suffering you have endured. What came out of those experiences?

Believe me, I know that struggling and suffering is hard. Despair and hopelessness are likely to set in during these times. These emotions are excruciating and they can make you feel like you will never feel better again.

Here's the truth as I know it. Suffering is a vital part of life. Let that sink in. Struggle is one of the most valuable teachers if we are willing and ready to learn.

We must suffer and struggle in order to experience the depth and breadth of an abundant life. Without the depths of despair, we will never truly know the heights of great joy. Without struggle we will never appreciate the ease of a peaceful life. We have to be intimately acquainted with both ends of the spectrum—and everything in between—in order to feel the emotional range life offers.

Some would argue that they can reach joy without having to suffer. They would insist that they can feel joy-filled without ever having to go through anything hard. I would respectfully disagree. Without the depths, you never have to really get to know your strength. If you've never had to sit with pain and decide to pull yourself out from the pit of suffering, you are merely living a surface level life. Surface level will never satisfy. It may seem alluring, but the glamour will always wear off. Trust me.

Pain grows us in ways that nothing else in life can. It forces us to become the person we were made to be—fully self-aware. We cannot truly and completely "know thyself" without walking through tough times. We would be utterly lopsided and it sounds harsh, but we would be very superficial.

Who wants that? Not me. I have walked through some intense trauma, but if you asked me today if I would change any of it—my answer would be a confident no. I would not change a single second. I would not be the person I am today, doing the work I am doing— writing this book—and helping others toward self-love had I not been through great trauma and heartache.

It all gave me perspective. It helped me to become a compassionate and empathetic witness to others' lives. It forced me to learn grace for myself and others. It compelled me to live a life of depth and meaning rather than skimming life's surface.

It's like buying your first car. When you have saved and sacrificed and waited so long to be able to buy the car for yourself, the purchase is so much sweeter. You care for the car in ways that wouldn't if it were just handed to you. It's like your baby. You know what it took to get it and you do everything you can to take care of it. Without the sacrifice, there is no meaning. It is just another material possession.

Be the hero of your story by choosing gratitude for the pain and suffering that you have endured. Forgive those that may have hurt you—thank them for what they taught you. Accept the things of the past and present that have caused you pain. Recognize the lessons and how strong you have become through times of struggle. This is the ultimate path to discovering self-love. You simply won't get there any other way.

That's not to say that you should sit in your suffering forever and keep people around that hurt you. Quite the opposite. As you grow in self-awareness and self-love, you will learn to accept the lessons of suffering and move on—you won't wallow or build up resentment. You will see it for what it is, let go, and move on. Same goes for people who have hurt you. You will learn to thank them for what they taught you, forgive them, and release them. When you have reached this place of power, life will have a richness that makes all of your experiences—even the bad—so worth it. You won't wish anything away. You will see very clearly that it all mattered. It all made you who you are today.

The Biological Purpose of Pain

The human body creates pain signals to alert the rest of the body that something needs attention. Oftentimes, we feel pain as the body's immune system rushes to the injured area to help it heal. Then as healing occurs, the pain dissipates. Our body then goes into clean-up mode, ridding the body of all of the by-products of the injury. And usually, the pain is gone soon enough—and we're healed.

In many cases, emotional pain isn't as evident as physical pain but it is just as painful—if not more—and should be treated with great care. When we have an emotional injury, we must to tend to it. We need to dissect the emotions attached to it, and boil them down to things we can understand. Then we need to process it, learn from it, and clean it up. Emotional clean-ups are just as important as the last step of physical healing.

There are no shortcuts in emotional healing. You cannot leave your emotional wounds half-healed. Band-Aid approaches will never heal wounds. This will simply cover them and allow them to fester and invade the area around the wound. Eventually you will need a bigger Band-Aid—and this will go on infinitely until you are ready to peel back the layers of Band-Aids and truly examine and heal your wounds.

Emotional pain shouldn't—and doesn't have to—define you; it should enlighten you and teach you what it means to have joy. It should make you more self-aware of your power. And most of all, it should teach you compassion, grace, forgiveness, and empathy. The only person who can save you from emotional pain is you—by doing the work and loving yourself out of it. When you want personal growth, self-love is the way to get through the pain and discover the myriad lessons available to you. You will become a deeper and more feeling being. Your life will take on new meaning and purpose. A life well-examined is a life well-lived.

Do the work. It's so worth it!

Learning the Hard Way

For some reason, most of us tend to learn lessons the hard way. For me, learning through the pain gave me the moment of clarity I needed to overcome domestic violence. I realized I hadn't finished my emotional clean-up, so I hadn't taken the time to understand my pain. Therefore, I repeatedly let the same pain come back and hurt me, over and over.

Personally, I don't think learning a lesson the hard way is a failure in any way. If you've allowed the same person, place, or situation to repeatedly hurt you, trust me when I say that you aren't alone. Sometimes, lessons can't be learned until we're ready. And other times, it takes a while. We cannot learn unless we can identify that there's a lesson to learn. And that's okay. The important thing is that when you come to the moment when you realize that your pain exists, you give yourself the chance to heal.

It took me a long time to learn certain lessons in my life. But no one can rush the process, and we don't learn until we're ready. In fact, the specific lesson I'm about to share with you took me years to learn.

After my dad left that fateful morning, I always imagined he'd return. I knew it wasn't a realistic thought, but some small part of me still had hope that our family would be together and we would be happy again someday. I held onto that hope for years.

Somehow, as my dad distanced himself more and more from my family, I became more and more attached to the idea that he'd come back into my life, and be the father figure I had memories of as a young child. And I think he did, too, in his own small, twisted way. Don't get me wrong; my dad is not a bad man. He's made some decisions that have hurt myself and my family, and I'm sure there are many things he isn't proud of. But he didn't do them to hurt us. He's simply so hurt inside that he can't be a positive force in any-one's life. I made this clarification because what I'm about to say will surely break some of your hearts.

For years after my dad left, he would occasionally call and text me to tell me he was going to come visit. I would be ecstatic. I would make sure I was wearing nice, clean, pressed clothes, and that my room was in order. I would mentally prepare all the things I wanted to tell him about: the basketball trophy I'd won, and the good grades I'd gotten in school. Then I'd wait.

Eagerly sitting in front of my window, I would wait and wait and wait and wait. The afternoon sun would retire, and the gentle evening moon would rise. And I'd still be waiting.

I know it broke my mother's heart. She'd come in and tell me that he wasn't coming, and that I should move away from the window. But I would fiercely disagree, "He told me he was coming to get me."

He never showed up. Later, I found out that he was frequently in another country when he told me he was coming to see me. He never had any intention of seeing me. Yet again and again, I let this same broken promise hurt me.

But on one occasion, he actually did come, and it was even on my birthday. I thought to myself, "Wow, he must be changing. He must be getting better. He's here on my birthday." I got into his car, and was so excited to see him. Then I found out he had no clue it was my birthday; it was a coincidence that he came that day. Yet somehow, I rationalized that all my birthday wishes had finally come true. By some miracle, he was there on my birthday, even though he had no clue it was that day.

As I said before, some lessons are harder to learn than others. Because I had so many emotional attachments to this particular lesson, it took me years of pain to learn that I could let that wound heal. I didn't want to learn this lesson, even though it became clearer that I needed to heal after every disappointment.

There's one universal factor for emotional healing: It takes time. I had to understand the heartbreak I attached to each experience, and figure out why it caused me so much pain. Here are the reasons I came up with:

- I was hurt that he broke his promise to me.

- I was angry that I fell for his lies, over and over.

- I felt incomplete when I realized I would never have a father figure in my life.

- Most of all, I didn't understand how someone I loved so much couldn't show up for me.

After I wrote that list, I sat with it in my hand and looked at my handwriting. I realized I needed to heal from a lot of pain. I chewed on each reason as long as I needed to, so I could finally find peace. It wasn't easy, but in the end, I made peace with myself and my dad.

The Lessons I Learned

After I allowed myself to heal, here's what I learned:

1. **I couldn't heal until I admitted to myself I'd experienced the pain.**

   Sometimes, this lesson is the hardest one to learn. As long as you can ignore the pain and shove it in a corner where it doesn't take up space, you can function, be happy, and think you're moving on. But like anything else, we can't ignore these wounds forever.

2. **I couldn't heal until I took responsibility for my pain.**

   Now some of you may be thinking, "How could you take responsibility for your pain when someone else hurt you?" Simple. I allowed my expectations to hurt me. When he didn't show up, I experienced pain because I placed expectations on him. I told myself that if he didn't show up it was because he didn't love me—because I wasn't good enough.

   Through healing, I learned that a big part of the pain I felt was self-inflicted. When I understood that his actions reflected where he was in his life and that it had nothing to do with me, I was able to let go of a large chunk of that pain.

3. **I couldn't heal until I learned that forgiveness is for me, not for the person I'm forgiving.**

Buddha says that holding onto a piece of hot coal only hurts you, not the person who handed it to you. The same is true for holding onto pain. Forgiving means you've taken the time to break down the emotions attached to the pain, learned a lesson from it, and chosen to let it go. I had to forgive my dad for not being the father I so desperately needed him to be.

4. I couldn't heal until I let my wounds fully heal.

You cannot rush the process. In the beginning, some wounds heal quickly, but it takes a while for that scar to fade. It's occasionally okay to revisit the pain, and readdress the parts that may still need tending to. Remember, healing is a process, and maintenance is a huge part of the process.

Loving from Afar

Nowadays, I love my dad from afar. We don't have much contact. But it's so important to learn that loving someone sometimes means keeping your distance. The person you love may not be good for your happiness, but you don't have to stop loving them. However, you do need to heal and set healthy boundaries, so the person doesn't fracture your happiness or peace of mind.

Pain happens, but growth is optional. Remember, no healing can occur when you're in an emotional black hole. You have to choose to utilize your pain to become a catalyst for deeper understanding, and a time to heal. Everyone won't understand your pain. In fact, some may think your pain is trivial or unnecessary, and that you're choosing to feel it. But your truth is the only key to making sense of your pain; it allows you to have the chance to learn and heal as a better, stronger, more self-aware human being.

Minds Like Rivers

When I was first facing the pain of my father's ongoing abandonment, a wise old woman once told me that sadness and pain need to be welcomed into our conscious minds. "We need to be like rivers," she said. At the time, I was dumbfounded by this statement. *How can my mind be like a river? Why would I invite unpleasant feelings into my thoughts?*

I remember the next thing she said as if it happened yesterday: "In order to heal, you have to be able to let all your emotions flow through you. If you try to run or hide from pain and sadness, they'll get trapped inside you, and you'll have no way out. Your subconscious mind will become a prisoner to these negative feelings, and they'll keep haunting until you choose to acknowledge them in your conscious mind. So invite all your emotions in, thank them for their existence, and let them move through you."

While learning to love myself, I've reminded myself of her words time and time again. All experiences aren't great; some of them are even painful beyond reason. But there's always something to be learned, beyond all the pain you feel. Have the courage to face yours, and know that you're allowing yourself to get better by doing so.

It's so hard to do, but on this journey to self-love, it's imperative to learn to be grateful for the lessons we learn during the hard times. This gratitude involves putting your ego aside, and not playing the victim.

If there is pain, there is growth to be gained—regardless of the situation, and who or what is involved. Why are you hurting? How will you behave differently next time, to prevent a similar situation from occurring again? Did you do something wrong, hurt someone else, and inadvertently hurt yourself in the process? Did someone wrong you that you thought you could trust?

Any of these reasons could be true, and trust me, I know pain sometimes swallows you whole. But when you finally decide that enough is enough, you get up and keep moving, which is when growth happens. In painful situations, you reveal your true strength to yourself. Sure, sometimes it's not as neat and pretty as you would have hoped, but you can find immense strength in the self-awareness you find after going through a painful experience.

Take the time to dissect exactly what caused you pain, learn the lessons, be gentle and kind to yourself and others, and let it go.

Summary of Growth

Take a moment, and write down three things that are still causing you pain.

Have them? Now repeat after me:

"I accept this pain. I know it hurts because it matters to me. I have healing to do, and I'm ready to become stronger and more self-aware as a result of this pain. The more I choose to understand myself, the more I love myself for everything I am. Pain doesn't control me or break me, because I've chosen growth."

Take a deep breath in and let it out... You are on the right path. Your journey has begun. Your truest self awaits. You will be awestruck by the beauty that unfolds!

Selflovology Tips for Growth

- Fill your life with people who encourage growth, not pain.

- If you experience pain, use it as a way to grow. When you believe in yourself, you start embracing the struggle.

- When someone hurts you, reflect on why you're allowing it.

- Learn to let go of the causes of the pain, and know when it's time to walk away.

- Recognize your self-worth, and stop hurting yourself.

- During your lowest times, go back to your gold-dot moment, and hold onto it.

Chapter 9

Outgrowing People

"If I have resistance to something, it means there's something wrong. The resistance to me is a sign of fear."

Billy Corgan

Growth involves resistance. It may sound counterintuitive, but it's true. Most human beings have a natural tendency to lean away from change because it's, well, new. We are routine-driven creatures that love the security of predictable outcomes. Armed with knowledge, it's reasonable to believe that some people who you're close to now may push back as you develop into a more refined, aware version of yourself.

Here's the fact of the matter: Nothing is more uncomfortable than people who are unwilling to adapt when someone close to them changes. Become comfortable with that fact, but don't let it deter you from what you want and need in your own life.

The people that truly matter will cheer you on and eventually may walk this path of self-love. The people who resist—they will naturally fall away. And that's okay.

Options

As we grow up, an interesting phenomenon occurs. Some of us have children. Some of us start a business and get married. Some of us travel the world, then finally settle in a far-off place we never would have imagined we'd end up. And some of us stay young forever, keep dating, have no interest in settling down, and enjoy living just as we always have.

There is no right or wrong way of living, and we each have our own choices to make about what completes us and makes us happy. However, it's important to realize that just because your best friends are choosing one life path, it may not be your life path. Again, that's okay.

In our lives, we will naturally grow closer to some people, and more distant from others. Who we align with, changes, depending on where we are in our own lives. That best friend you had in elementary school may no longer share your common interests, and that's okay. Yes, you were once inseparable and now live completely different lives, but that doesn't mean either one of you did anything wrong. You may simply not understand each other anymore, since you're in different places in life and want different things.

Respect yourself and others in your life enough to know when to let people go. You can love and respect someone, and not have them in your day-to-day life. You shouldn't stop growing because someone else doesn't understand your journey and process. They will only slow you down and keep you looking in the rearview mirror.

I've seen this time and time again: People are afraid to grow because they're afraid of what will happen to their relationships with their friends, family, and significant others. But the truth is that people either grow in the same direction with you, or in a different direction. In other words, you either grow together, or you grow apart.

You cannot fear the outcome, but it is important that you find peace about this reality of life.

Also, it's important to recognize that this goes both ways.

This same truth and grace of letting go applies to others letting you go. If people around you are growing in a direction that you are not yet ready for, or a place you're not interested in going, it's okay if those people choose to let you go. Again, it doesn't mean they don't love and respect you, it just means the course of your time together has come to a fork in the road.

It's all okay. People come and go like the seasons. Eventually, you will find your tribe of people that are your forever people. They are living lives that reflect your heart's desires and your passions. These people spur you on and keep you on the path of further growth and self-love.

It's important for me to note that I am not suggesting that you live in a bubble. I am not suggesting that you only surround yourself with people just like you. Quite the opposite. I am suggesting you find people who make you want to be a better version of yourself. That doesn't mean you think exactly the same way or act the same way—these people simply are in alignment with their own selves so they are able inspire you to do the same for yourself.

Please do surround yourself with all sorts of people. Expose yourself to different beliefs, religions, ways of living, etc. Doing so will only help you to refine your own set of beliefs and how you live your life.

Blameless Growth

For example, consider your significant other. For the purposes of this chapter, let's say your partner is a man named Connor.

In the beginning, you and Connor are inseparable. You both just graduated from college and got your first jobs in your fields. Life is good. You both work 9-5 and enjoy grabbing a drink with your friends in the evenings. On the weekends, you relax, go grocery shopping, and get ready for the next week together. Things seem like they couldn't get any better. You start thinking about how wonderful it would be to spend the rest of your lives together, so you start discussing marriage.

Time goes by. You both work the same number of hours, but somehow, you spend less time together. After work, you go out with your coworkers, and come home tired and ready for bed. But Connor has been home since he got off work. He's in the bedroom reading a new book, and is excited when you get home because he wants to tell you what he did and learned that day. However, you had a long day, and you already vented and decompressed with your work friends. So, you brush him off and go to bed.

That weekend, you want to go to a talk about a subject you're interested in, and the speaker is only in town that weekend. But Connor would rather go to the beach and BBQ with his friends until the sun goes down. Things aren't perfect, but they aren't bad.

Time passes, and you find a new job that allows you to truly follow your passion. Then you realize that it's no longer enough for you to allow your job to be your main identity. You want more: a hobby or something to pursue that brings out a passion you haven't felt in a while.

Meanwhile, Connor is perfectly content where he is, and doesn't see a problem with it. His job pays well enough, and he still enjoys going out with his friends and living the life you used to enjoy together. But that life is no longer enough for you. You feel like Connor is lacking purpose and passion, and it takes a toll on the relationship.

I want to pause here for a minute and ask: Is there anything wrong with either one of the people in this relationship? The answer is no; they simply want different things. You want more, but Connor is happy with the life he has. No one is to blame, but the relationship is no longer working. It's so easy to place blame in relationships, but it's not the solution.

No Change = No Change

Life won't always keep the same people by our sides.

Some people are meant to be in your life for a season, and others come into your life for a specific reason. In order to align with your life path, you need to know when it's time to move on, and be on your own. This rule of thumb is true for both romances and friendships, and it certainly won't be easy. But fear is never a good reason to stay. We're all destined for better futures than that.

If you've outgrown someone, do yourself a favor, and stop fighting so hard for something that isn't meant to be in your life. Instead of holding on and trying to change other people, let them go and move on with grace and purpose.

There will always be people you want to stay in your life, but who simply cannot exist in it. However, moving on doesn't necessarily mean that someone will stop being a regular part of your life for all eternity. There is no end to our growth. So sometimes, the people who fall out of our lives may rejoin us at another point along our journey, after their trajectory realigns with ours.

As you grow, you'll learn that if nothing changes—nothing changes. And if you aren't willing to let go of things to get where you're going—you'll never get anywhere.

Tree in the Rainforest

First and foremost, your responsibility is to yourself. If you aren't good for yourself, you cannot be good for anyone else, including your significant other, your children, and your friends. You need to come to terms with the fact that growth means moving forward.

Growth will always mean leaving some things and people in the past and keeping your gaze toward the future. This is not a bad thing.

If you're struggling with coming to terms with this concept, use this example: You're a tree in the rainforest. You're small, and there are other small trees around you. But your foundation is strong, and you have all you need. So you spread your roots and start growing.

As you grow, animals come nest in your branches. At first, there are birds, then frogs and lizards. You are abundant, so you can provide homes for them all. They rely on you for shelter, and live off the raindrops and dew that collects on your leaves. But as you grow, you notice the other trees around you. Some are growing with you, but others simply aren't thriving in the same way.

They seem to be getting weaker as you get stronger. And as you grow, you start casting bigger and bigger shadows on them as you tower over them. You cannot stop your growth. It's not up to you anymore.

You want to help the smaller, weaker trees, but you can't. You cannot give them more nourishment, more room, or more light. You're growing, and they're not. There's no stopping nature. As you get larger and larger, you completely block the sunlight from reaching the trees below. You're thriving, and there's no slowing down.

When you remove choice from the equation, things are simple. The tree has no choice but to grow. However, human beings allow misguided emotions to overcomplicate things. We somehow connect growth with abandonment. We think that because we can choose to stay the same, we have to feel guilt for outgrowing our surroundings. Since we view growth as a choice, we create a crisis in ourselves, even though it doesn't matter in reality.

Just like the tree, we deserve to thrive, and we aren't harming anyone or anything by becoming better. It's a choice we make, and we can't bear the burden of guilt for those around us that don't make the same choices as us.

The Captain of Your Own Ship

Here's a difficult truth that people often struggle with: Sometimes, we have to learn to love people from afar. Just because you're in a different place in your life than someone you love, you don't necessarily have to lose that person. You can support them, spend time with them, and even find things you both relate to. But that doesn't mean you should slow your growth down for someone else.

Remember, your primary responsibility is to yourself, and no one else. If life is taking you down a path that you know is important for you to explore, then explore it. You're in charge of your life.

If that path turns out to be the wrong one, it's okay. You can always turn around and choose a new path. When we're growing and developing, we somehow get the idea that all our decisions are finite. But that's not the case: Everything is constantly changing.

Growth isn't always going to have a linear, upward trajectory. Sometimes, things are messy, and the line of growth looks more like a jagged edge than a straight line. The point is not how fast we grow and how far we go, but rather the effort we make and the awareness we have about our own growth and trajectory.

Here's the bottom line: You never have to feel guilty about what is good and right for you, even if your path takes some twists and turns.

You don't have to be right to justify your growth. You don't have to feel guilty when you're wrong about what you thought you wanted. It's all part of your growth. It won't be perfect, and I'm sure you'll frequently be tempted to throw in the towel and go back to the familiar, just like everyone else.

But there's no growth in that. If you want something better, you need to trust yourself and allow yourself to explore what this growth might mean for you. The right people will always appear to help you grow, so stop worrying about trying to explain your journey to someone who's not ready to understand it.

As you grow into your own best version of yourself, you'll start attracting people who are similar to you. When you stop forcing friendships and relationships to evolve and allow yourself to align with yourself, you'll soon find that you'll find a surplus of people who are vibrating at your frequency.

Summary of Moving On

Let's jump back to the tree in the rainforest. The largest trees make up the canopy of the forest. There's no need to compete, since there's enough sunlight to go around. There's no scarcity or lack of nourishment.

As you grow, you'll find people who are also growing. You'll align yourself with people who make you better, who challenge you, and who don't want to stunt your growth. These people are basking in their own portion of light. There is no competition. You are growing in tandem.

Trust your process. Know that for every person who pushes back, you will push yourself one more step toward your dream life. Stop wasting your time on the people who:

- Don't support your dreams.

- Steal your energy, rather than energize you.

- Feed fear and lock you into a place that you know doesn't serve you.

For a moment, I want you to eliminate guilt, fear, and feelings about being responsible for other people's happiness. Would you still be in the place you're in now, or would you be running toward something better?

If you answered that you'd be doing something different, then you've just given yourself the answer. And you just had a breakthrough. Congratulations! You just realized that you're shackled by your limiting beliefs and misplaced emotional sludge.

Ultimately, you deserve to follow your own path. Now it's time to get moving. Stop limiting your vision to make sure everyone in your life is comfortable with it. Set yourself free by knowing that you're allowed to outgrow others and move on. And accept that some may outgrow you and let you go. It's all good. It means everyone is working toward getting better. It doesn't have to be a parallel experience. If everyone followed this advice, how much more advanced would the world be? Unleash your potential, and stop apologizing for what you want.

Selflovology Tips for Moving On

- Pinpoint what makes you uncomfortable.

- Respect yourself enough to accept when it's time to move on. Remember, some people are only meant to be in your life for a short period of time.

- Don't avoid opportunities or stop growing to please someone else. Outgrowing someone might be messy, but it's also often necessary.

- Moving on means being true to you. So be the change you want to see in your life.

Chapter 10

Self-Love, Together

> *"Real love amounts to letting a person be what he really is."*
>
> **Jim Morrison**

No one can make you happy. No one's love is going to make you feel less broken. A relationship cannot save you or make you happy. All of these things are your responsibility—no one else's.

I would be lying if I said I never believed that another person would somehow make me whole, or that my happiness was directly related to another person's actions. In fact, these truths are some of the hardest ones to face. It's always easier to look outside ourselves for solutions than to face them and find love, happiness, and fulfillment through the process of self-healing and self-love.

Organizing Your Baggage

The last time you went to the airport, how many different types of bags did you see? We all have baggage. Like the various kinds of bags you'd see at an airport, your emotional baggage is indicative of your life experience. Some of us have more baggage than others. Some of our baggage has wheels, so it effortlessly glides along as we walk. For others, it's heavy and makes your shoulders sore as you lug it with you everywhere you go.

All of these types of baggage are okay. They make us complex, human, compassionate, and unique. But for every type of baggage, there's some things we can unpack and there are easier ways to carry it.

When we are truly healthy and living from a place of self-love, we realize we don't actually have to carry our baggage. We learn that we can put it in its place—only returning to it when we have deeper lessons to learn or more self-awareness to gain.

It can be as neat and tidy as we make it and over time if we are doing the real work of self-love, our baggage will be unnecessary to our continued growth. When it's time we can actually thank the baggage for helping carry our loads and then simply discard the bags.

Let me break some of this down for you in a practical way. Imagine that you're moving into a new home, and you have to select bags to carry all of your life belongings from your old house to your new house. You can choose a nice, matching set of luggage with compartments, shiny zippers, and wheels. Or you can choose the old duffle bags buried in the back of your closet. The zipper is broken, so you can't make sure your stuff won't fall out as you move it. And the bags don't have wheels, just old straps that look like they're ready to break.

Which bags would you choose to move your most important possessions in? The obvious answer is the shiny new set of luggage that will protect your belongings, won't break your back, and won't cause everything to fall out in transit.

Use the same concept to bring your baggage into relationships. Do you want to be in a relationship with someone who is lugging around baggage that is unorganized and tattered, and spills out over the top? Or do you want to be with someone who has everything nicely packed and in its place?

Before you say I want to be with the person who has zero baggage, let me tell you that's a great goal but likely not possible at this stage in your life. Ask yourself if you have baggage. This will be very telling. You can't expect to find someone without baggage if you are still working on unpacking your own.

In order to find yourself in a happy, healthy relationship, you must learn how to organize your own baggage. You need to make peace with who and what you are. And most importantly, you need to learn how to digest and heal your emotional baggage, so it won't spill over into your relationships.

In a healthy and happy relationship, you must take the time to come to peace with the baggage you bring into it, so you won't project those wounds onto a new relationship.

Also, this is an important piece about baggage: Keep your hands off other people's baggage. This is the adult version of "keep your hands to yourself." You cannot help other people organize and clear out their baggage. That is not your role and this will only set up a relationship riddled with co-dependency.

It will be tempting, believe me. You will see things that you've already worked through and you'll want to swoop in and save the day. You are not here to save other people. This is not your place.

Keep your hands on your own baggage.

Like Attracts Like

Without having self-love and self-awareness, you'll never feel fully fulfilled in your relationships, because there's a fundamental piece missing: yourself. Furthermore, you won't be able to experience a healthy, functional, long-lasting relationship until you stop counting on others to fix or save you. Remember, your partner can't even see half of the things you think need to be saved.

In order to foster complete acceptance, you need to learn to accept yourself. You shouldn't change for a relationship, in the hopes the relationship will change you. If you don't know yourself, you'll be more likely to struggle in your relationships, because no one else can know you either.

Self-hatred is contagious. So, if you're in a relationship with someone who doesn't love themselves, the feeling will spread into your interactions with one another, no matter how hard you try to fix that person.

Cleaning House

There comes a point when we need to take responsibility for our own lives and become our own advocates. In order to be in a self-loving relationship with another person, you may have to refuse to accept your partner's lack of growth. Along this journey, it's okay to outgrow people, so don't let that get you down. When you act better, you attract better, and you'll soon see why self-love is so paramount in a relationship.

We've all experienced the feeling of wanting the best for someone we love. But we may forget what's best for us in the process. And no, it's not selfish to want what's best for yourself, especially when it involves your mental capacity, peace of mind, or stress.

You have to work on yourself, even if:

- You're in a relationship you're not happy in.

- Your partner is hurting you in some way.

- You're searching for a relationship because you feel lonely, but you're unable to find someone.

Why are you accepting being with someone who's treating you less than? Why are you so desperate for a relationship that you'll take anyone who comes around?

It's your choice. How do want your life to be? Until you decide you want betterness for yourself and choose self-love, you'll only find toxic relationships filled with drama and miscommunication. A loving relationship doesn't include abuse, condescension, or deception.

There's a reason you're attracting bitterness and toxicity. It's not about them. If you want to be better, you have to choose better. This truth is the same for everyone: If you want to be in a relationship full of love, honesty, and integrity, you need to embody those qualities. And if you focus on a quality within yourself, you'll attract it into your life.

The length of time someone has been in your life shouldn't determine the length of time that you stay with them. You're fully capable of releasing anyone from your life who has continued to reveal themselves to be toxic and negative.

Being in Love with Yourself

Up until now, we've discussed why you can't have a long-lasting, healthy relationship if you don't love and know yourself. So you might be wondering what self-love looks like in a relationship.

Let's take a look at what it means to be in love with yourself, alongside another person. After finishing this chapter, you'll have a toolbox of wonderful tools that will help you make sure you're in a healthy relationship.

First, let's define self-love within the context of a relationship. Ironically, the best way to clarify this definition is to articulate what this context doesn't involve.

A relationship, especially a new one, can be a full-time job. As you get to know one another, there's so much to learn. There's even more to discuss and experience, so you can make sure the partnership is based on more than just physical attraction.

It can be easy to get lost in moments of bliss. And if you're not careful, you can become too much like your significant other, and lose yourself in the process of loving someone else. There's a fine line between learning alongside your partner, and learning to be more like your partner.

In order to enter a healthy, mutually beneficial relationship, it's imperative that both partners show up as themselves, and work together to create and maintain a healthy relationship that's based on love, respect, and communication.

Even if you and your partner are together in mind, body, and spirit, you're ultimately on your own journey. Rather than living one combined life, you are two completely separate entities who are sharing the experience of your lives together.

There's nothing wrong with wanting to be with your partner, but you shouldn't rely on them to be happy or feel like you can't live without them. Instead, you should enjoy their company, but be whole without them. There's a difference between love and codependency.

Sharing true self-love is a beautiful thing. In this type of relationship, several concepts are put into ongoing practice. If you're trying to create a self-love relationship with someone else, it's imperative that you've mastered the concept of self-awareness.

Communicating with Both Genders

Recalling the earlier section about facets, it's important to acknowledge that we all have a masculine side and a feminine side. You need to realize that you need to maintain a common balance, based on your understanding of who's speaking in each conversation.

For example, if a woman is speaking about her day at work, she's probably approaching it from her masculine side. So she needs different attention and feedback than she would if she was talking about shopping for a dress, which would be channeling her more feminine energy.

So develop an understanding of this concept, and cater the type of energy you give your partner accordingly. Then you'll help both parties feel complete and heard in a relationship.

In other words, being cognizant of this idea will further help you increase your self-awareness and understand what's being communicated. Then you can avoid unnecessary misunderstandings. As you can see, communicating with your significant other from a place of self-awareness is essential to fostering a healthy relationship.

Empathy vs Sympathy

Are you making your partner's problems your own burdens? Remember, a healthy partnership doesn't involve two people becoming one. Rather, it involves two people sharing their individual journeys and being together as separate beings. Each piece is whole, so it isn't dependent on the other to complete itself.

It can be easy to want to fix your partner, but remember that it's not your job. Learn how to give advice and support, without taking on your partner's burdens. It's much healthier to separate these two concepts.

I've frequently heard people say they feel like their partners control them, or that they resent them for certain things. These feelings boil down to one issue: You cannot grow on your own journey if you're living someone else's. In fact, if you try to live someone else's growth for them, you'll end up robbing them of their own healing journey.

Being in love and growing together means sharing, loving, and supporting. But it doesn't mean you're obligated to take on anyone else's struggles, pain, or growths. And it won't lead to a fulfilling relationship.

You can be a compassionate witness for all that your partner is walking through and they can be that for you in return. You don't have to get all up in their healing process in order to be helpful. Holding space and being a witness—showing them that they are seen and heard—is the most powerful and helpful gift you can offer.

A Sense of Trust

In order to trust your partner, you must first learn to trust yourself. You must learn to be self-aware, and heal any wounds from your past.

By learning how to heal yourself, you're learning self-love, so you can extend that love outwards to your partner in the form of true and long-lasting trust. When learning to trust yourself, you must forgive others and learn from your past actions and experiences, and you must allow space for your partner to do the same.

It's essential for you and your partner to do the inner work and come to a place where you can share a sacred bond of trust. Each of you needs to be self-aware and secure about your identity and your worth.

A Respectful Atmosphere

Last but most certainly not least, you must learn to respect yourself and your journey. You cannot expect another person to respect you if you aren't extending that same kindness to yourself. Be aware of your internal banter, speak positively to yourself, and respect your mind and body every day.

By respecting yourself, you're setting the precedent for the way you'll be treated. Until I learned this lesson, I didn't understand that my abusive ex-girlfriend was physically treating me the way I was mentally treating myself. In order to foster mutual respect, you must first respect yourself.

Summary of Togetherness

Being in a relationship focused on self-love is exactly the way it sounds: It's based on two people understanding and loving themselves and their unique processes, and choosing to share them with one another.

Remind yourself that you can choose the people you want to be in a relationship with. You don't have to stay in a relationship that doesn't operate on the principles of self-love. There's nothing shameful or selfish about setting standards for yourself, and making your intentions and standards known.

You'll know that the right person has come into your life through the following criteria:

- You love yourself through it all.

- You don't lose yourself or get hurt.

- You don't give up on the love that matters most: self-love.

Your participation in relationships starts with holding yourself accountable, which means working towards self-love every day and spreading it throughout your daily life.

To me, soulmates are two individuals who fully love themselves. They're intimately connected with their own souls, so they're open to sharing all aspects of themselves to the people they're attracted to. With full transparency on both sides and a desire for continued personal development, you can develop an incredible relationship based on self-love.

Let go of the idea of "you complete me..."

Who wants that? This suggests that you are not whole and the only way you will ever be whole is if someone else comes into your life. This is so damaging.

Let's change the narrative. Rather than "you complete me," let's learn to say "you are working toward becoming complete for yourself and so am I. Together we will be two complete beings complementing and supporting one another along the way."

Yes, this feels right. This feels true.

Selflovology Tips for Togetherness

- Love yourself enough to surround yourself with like-minded people.

- Instead of dwelling on the hurt people have caused you in the past, focus on choosing better people for your life now.

- Don't settle for less. Release people from your life who are negatively weighing you down.

- Remember you are the love of your life, so be the type of person you want to have in your life. By being your best you, you will improve every other relationship.

- Show the world you love yourself, so you'll attract people who love you. If you don't have self-love, you cannot love anyone else.

Chapter 11

Setting Boundaries

"Don't compromise yourself. You're all you have."

John Grisham

Until you learn how to set your own boundaries, people will keep pushing them. Setting boundaries can mean different things to different people. In the context of self-love, setting boundaries means setting a code of conduct for yourself, and sticking with it. It means learning when to say no to people, places, and things that don't feel right to you.

You should set boundaries for all kinds of relationships (including romantic, business, and family). In my experience, people struggle with setting boundaries more than anything else. It's so easy to fall into this cycle: trying to please everyone, and compromising your own health and wellbeing for the sake of other people. I've often seen people become confused about the difference between compromising their boundaries for the people they love, and being a good friend, spouse, or parent.

The Boundary List

Let's do an exercise together, so you'll have a chance to create and explore the boundaries you'd like to create in your life.

First off, let's define the word "boundary." Merriam-Webster defines a boundary as "a line that marks the limits of an area; a dividing line, a limit of a subject or sphere of activity." Now that we understand what the word means, let's apply it to your life.

Take a moment to list some boundaries you already have. Don't just think about them; write them down. In a relationship, what's a deal-breaker for you? Do you tolerate cursing in your workplace? Do you accept an invasion of privacy at home? The next time you arrive at a place where you have to set boundaries in a relationship, this list will be a powerful tool.

It can be easy to change boundaries with people we aren't very close to. But it's often more difficult to maintain them with the people we love most. What happens with these people? We waver, and allow that person to be the exception to the rule.

The truth is that there should be no exceptions to the code of conduct you have for your life. As hard as it may sound, everyone you have in your life should respect your boundaries. And if someone disrespects them once, they'll probably do it over and over again.

Here's the point: No matter how much a person means to you, they don't respect you if they don't respect your basic boundaries. Oftentimes, writing out boundaries will keep you accountable, so you won't allow people to come into your life that you know won't respect the things that bring you peace.

Remember, when you allow someone to curve your boundary line, you show them how to treat you. The only things in our lives are the things we allow to be there. So if you're strong and stand by what you believe in, the people who matter to you will respect you for respecting yourself.

The Roots of Boundaries

Now that you have your list, let's take it a step further, and investigate why you've set these boundaries. What made you write them down? What does it mean to you if your boundaries aren't respected? Be specific.

For example, one boundary involves cursing: I don't use curse words, and I don't allow others to use them if they're directed at me.

I've set this boundary for myself. To me, this boundary is important because I don't feel safe if someone directs that language at me. Since I don't feel the person is in a place where he or she can rationally discuss anything, I no longer want to communicate with that person. Therefore, I remove myself from any and all people who choose to direct curse words at me. I do not need this language in my life, since it does not make me feel good. So I've chosen to cut it out of my life.

Now take a moment to delve into the reasons why your boundaries exist. What experiences have made you choose these specific items? Why are they important to you? Again, write them down. Being able to refer to why they matter to you will help you uphold them in your life.

The Boundary Map

Finally, I want you to lay your boundaries down in your life. Imagine them like streets that lead to your house. How do we give directions? We tell people where to turn, what intersections to look for, where to be careful, and what to expect if they drive too far.

Now that they're well-defined, there will be no surprises to those who are close to you. You're clear about where you stand, so they use the roadmap you've created to get to your house, and know exactly which roads to take. By defining our boundaries, we aren't being rude or stubborn, and we aren't exhibiting any other negative attributes that we may have previously attributed to the necessary lines we must draw.

The Power of Choice

By creating, defining, and laying down boundaries, we've taken the guesswork out of the relationships we're in. And we can exist with a common understanding, yet without expectations or coercions.

People will either choose to respect your boundaries, or they won't. And just as they have a choice, you also have the choice to accept the boundaries that are being overstepped, or to walk away. And yes, you are allowed to walk away from someone who doesn't respect your boundaries. It doesn't matter if that person is a family member, best friend, or spouse.

You are allowed to remove someone from your life who knows your boundaries, but chooses to overstep them. It's up to you to choose how you're going honor your boundaries. But regardless of your tactics, it's important to remember that they're choices. You're allowed to say no to things that don't serve you well. You're allowed to cut ties with people who don't help you step into a new season and bloom. Blood ties aren't deeper than self-respect, unless you allow them to be.

Boundary setting is a huge part of self-care, self-love, and maturity. Setting boundaries is showing love and care for yourself and acknowledging your needs and desires for that which surrounds your life. Boundaries are healthy. Too many times people think of boundaries as walls—keeping others out and imprisoning the boundary keeper.

Nothing could be further from the truth. Boundaries are clear guidelines, but they are not walls. They are clearly drawn lines created to protect ourselves and others in our lives. They show people how to treat us and they encourage others to create their own healthy boundaries in their lives.

Boundaries, like self-love, are contagious. People quickly see the effect of healthy boundaries—maintenance of core beliefs, mindful ways of moving throughout the world, meaningful relationship building, impactful experiences—and they want what they see for themselves. It is a practice that will make the world a better place.

Set healthy and strong boundaries. Respect yourself first, and others second.

A Rough Start

A huge part of stepping into self-love is becoming comfortable with the idea that some people won't understand your growth. And based on my own personal experience, this lack of understanding will include some of the people who are closest to you. Regardless of the size of the growth, it isn't always well-received. So in the beginning, it will be hard and so many will not understand.

You will have days when you question your new decision-making. But I need you to remember that anyone who doesn't want to see you become the best version of yourself isn't the best person for you. You need people in your life who are lifting you up during this time of life-change, not people who are criticizing and questioning. There will be many days of self-doubt and the allure of the way you used to live your life will be strong and attractive when things get tough.

These aren't signs that you should turn around and go back to the reality you knew before you made the decision. Rather, they're signs that you have to be clear about your boundaries. You have to make sure the people you love know exactly where you stand, and what you want in your life.

To what extent should you uphold your own boundaries? These limits will show others exactly how to treat you. If you aren't clear about your own limits, no one will know how to treat you. In fact, you won't even know how to treat yourself.

Internal Boundaries

So far, we've covered ways to create and maintain boundaries between ourselves and the people in our lives. But what about boundaries within ourselves? Yes, we all have internal boundaries that need to be carefully modulated.

Thankfully, these internal boundaries aren't as hard to define, but they're equally hard to uphold. Think of your internal boundaries as a self-care practice. When your practice isn't well-respected or properly tended, you could end up feeling empty and burned out.

You see, we don't only have to say no to the people, places, and things that make us feel uncomfortable and steal our peace from the outside world. We also have to learn to be aware of our internal environment, and make sure we aren't over-stretching boundaries that are healthy for ourselves—mentally, physically, and psychologically.

Your Inner Mean Girl

If you're working yourself too hard and constantly practicing negative self-talk, you're doing things that don't bring you joy—because you tell yourself you have to. Therefore, you aren't respecting your self-care practice. Moreover, if you're picking up and carrying others' emotional sludge as your own burden, you're not practicing safe, healthy internal boundaries.

It's not healthy for you to do anything more or less than actions that feel mentally and physically good for yourself. We have the tendency to be our own biggest critics, and to always look at what we could have done better, rather than what we're doing well. And worst of all, we have the tendency to steal our own happiness with limiting thoughts and nonsensical statements such as:

- "That isn't possible for me."

- "I don't have time for that right now."

So how do you get to a place of having healthy internal boundaries for yourself, when your inner mean girl tries to trick you into overdoing, overstepping, and under-appreciating yourself?

Here are a few simple tools you can use to make sure you're internally balanced:

- **Be aware of your inner mean girl.**

The more you acknowledge her presence, the more you can sense when she's coming in to throw you off-balance.

- **Use your inner mean girl to your advantage.**

  Make sure her objective is to make sure other people respect your boundaries. And she'll quickly know if you don't.

- **Make sure you're aware of inner self-talk.**

  Regularly check in with yourself to make sure that what you're doing is giving you energy, not draining every last ounce of your battery.

- **Say no to things that don't sound good or appealing to you.**

  You don't have to do everything that's offered or available to you. Some people feel like they're failures if they're not constantly busy. That's your inner mean girl talking. You're not a failure for taking time for yourself and having the strength to define what too much is.

- **Regularly practice self-care.**

  If you tend to forget to take care of yourself or brush it off, schedule it into your calendar. It doesn't make you a bad parent, spouse, significant other, or friend if you take time to do something you love on a regular basis. You should be practicing self-care at least four days a week and at least an hour a day. Take time to recharge, and respect your own time and energy.

- **Don't allow others to change your mind.**

  You are you, and they are them. They cannot feel what you feel, think what you think, or be you—just like you can't be them. Do what's best for you, regardless of what others say. With well-defined internal boundaries, you're less open to suggestibility, so you're more at peace with the decisions you make.

If you make other people's problems your own burdens, you're being codependent, rather than caring. Other people's issues and plights are not yours to solve, fix, and carry around. You are only responsible for yourself, and if you take on anything beyond that, you'll be giving up energy that you could otherwise invest in yourself. Let it go, take responsibility for you, and let others do the same.

Summary of Boundaries

It's monumentally important to set boundaries, both within yourself and for the outside world. Imagine trying to get somewhere without any street signs, intersections, or roads. Would you ever be able to get where you're going? Eventually you will, but why resort to guesswork when the signs and roads can be neatly painted and paved?

When you have boundaries, you know your worth, and you value the people around you. In fact, you give them clear signs about the types of things that will either cause you to keep them in your life, or force you to move away from them.

Your limits can be strengths, not weaknesses—if you choose to respect them. And they will give you the peace to understand which actions to take, and the power to carry them when something enters your life that is trying to steal your peace.

Strong boundaries do not make you weak. Strong boundaries make you strong. They clarify your purpose and path in the world and clear the way for boundless growth in your life. Like a plant with strong roots, strong boundaries give you a powerful framework for putting down your own roots, sprouting, growth, blossoming and creating fertile soil for generations to come.

Selflovology Tips for Boundaries

- Write down the current boundaries you have, as well as the ones you need to implement.

- Define the ways your boundaries give your life direction.

- Create internal boundaries that foster self-love.

- Learn to say no, especially when you feel obligated. Walk away from people who don't respect you.

- Pay attention to which people overstep your boundaries.

- Remember, some people won't be comfortable with your growth.

Chapter 12

Balance Your Being

> *"Life is like riding a bicycle. To keep your balance,*
> *you must keep moving."*
>
> **Albert Einstein**

Personal growth isn't always linear. Some days, I just want to lie on my couch in my sweatpants and do nothing. And that's okay. And other times, I just want to be average. And that's okay, too.

Self-love and personal growth don't constantly occur in an upward line. We all have times when we simply just want to exist, and can't fathom doing more than we already are. No one expects you to excel nonstop, so you shouldn't expect it of yourself.

In order to avoid burnout, you have to discover ways to find balance in your being, and embrace them. In other words, you have to make room for everything you are in your life.

The Spectrum of Emotions

Oftentimes, people who are going through personal growth think they have to feed certain parts of their character and squish others, in order to reach the next plateau. They think they can't grow if parts of themselves exhibit jealousy, insecurity, or any other negative emotion. But this viewpoint simply isn't true.

There's room in your life for all of you. That's where self-acceptance comes in. How do I know? Because I've gone through the journey, and I love myself. But I'd be lying if I said I didn't feel a sting of self-doubt every now and then.

Feeling a normal spectrum of human emotions doesn't make you look bad, so you need to stop playing into that mentality. Your feelings (positive and negative) bring balance into your being. Your journey to self-love shouldn't involve outgrowing human emotions. However, it should help you arrive at a place where you can receive, reflect on, and modulate negative emotions, then respond appropriately.

Being self-aware and having self-love doesn't make you perfect. In fact, nothing in this life will ever let you be as perfect as you probably want to be in this present moment. So balance your being by letting yourself feel whatever you need to, when you need to. But don't let yourself get stuck in a negative emotion. Self-love teaches us to allow for all emotions, but to modulate our responses to them.

For example, consider something that used to make you jealous. You may not realize that you no longer have to feel jealous about it because you now know you're beautiful, filled with talent and amazing skills, and made of nothing but wonderful thoughts. While another person may cause you to feel what I call "less-than-ness," you are able to stop, recognize the emotion, remind yourself of everything you are, and acknowledge that it shouldn't stop you from feeling like you're an amazing person.

You are the gatekeeper of your emotions. You are in full control of balancing the good and the not so good. The range of emotions you feel is what makes you uniquely you. No other person in the entire world can ever be like you. Your emotions are a beautiful expression of your spirit and your soul.

Never condemn yourself or fall into negative self-talk because you aren't flying high all of the time. The human ability to move through a spectrum of emotions is extraordinary. Like a sliding scale, this movement to and fro makes you a deeply feeling person in a world that can be cold and callous.

Celebrate your range and depth of emotion. Give thanks that you are at a place in your life where you can feel your feelings, learn from them, and become a better person each day.

Focusing Your Balance

Balancing your being also pertains to allowing yourself to be good enough for yourself. The older I've gotten, the more I've realized that I could be doing so many things in this life. There are so many skills I could learn, places I could visit, and career opportunities I could pursue. But I simply don't have enough time or energy to do everything at once.

I'm not saying you should shrink your vision, but you also don't need to think of yourself as Superman to fall in love with yourself. It's so important for you to arrive at a place where you realize you're powerful enough to do just about anything in this world if you set your mind to it. But remember, you don't have to do everything.

Don't overwhelm yourself by comparing what you're doing to what others are doing. Instead, focus on what your passions are, and immerse yourself in the joy that comes from fulfilling your passions on a daily, weekly, and monthly basis. It's easy to get carried away, and compare ourselves to all the other people out there that we label as being just like us. We look at people all day long—at work, while we're grocery shopping, and while we're on social media.

And we often fall into the trap of these kinds of thoughts: "Well, he's a father of three, and he's a millionaire with a $90 haircut and a perfect manicure. Meanwhile, I don't have any children. I still can't get my hair to lay down, and I can't ever find time for a manicure." These thoughts are unfair, and they prevent you from balancing your being.

Instead of spending your time thinking about how others are "out-lifting you," focus your time on finding the balance in your life, doing what you love, and filling your different needs.

Over time, you will see these outward expressions as meaningless. The money, the perfect hair, the perfectly manicured life will no longer matter in the same way it once did. You will grow past the need for these material expressions.

Instead, you will crave the depth and breadth of a well-examined inward life—money, cars, and haircuts will be replaced with deep meaningful conversations, noticing the joy or pain on another's face, offering kind words to strangers... This is the better life. All of the material things will fall away. What will remain—and what matters above all else—are relationships. The relationship with yourself and your relationships with others will leave an imprint that can never be erased.

Maslow's Hierarchy of Needs

In order to reach our highest potential and be the best versions of ourselves, we need to systematically find balance. First, we need to meet our physical needs. Then after we've met them, we can move on to the psychological needs. And after those needs are met, we can focus on self-fulfillment.

Just like the theory of Maslow's hierarchy, we as humans need to fill our needs in the same way. We have career obligations, family obligations, and many other obligations that we need to fulfill, but when the time comes to fulfill our obligation to ourselves, we often find ourselves too tired.

But finding balance teaches you that this situation doesn't have to be the case. You don't always have to put yourself last, and leave yourself with only your leftover energy to take care of your other obligations. You are allowed to prioritize the things that matter to you.

For a minute, think about what your days look like. What do you do? Who do you do it for? And why? Do you maintain a planner for the things you have to do? If you do, do you allot time to do things for yourself?

When I talk about doing something for yourself, I'm not referring to grocery shopping. Instead, I'm talking about things that fill you up and give you the purpose and energy to do all the other wonderful things you do. If you don't, then you aren't giving yourself the chance to reach your highest potential. In order to achieve self-fulfillment and self-actualization, you have to allot enough time to yourself. By doing things that make you happy, you can develop a deeper self-love and understanding of yourself.

Summary of Balance

I've said it many times: To be the best version of yourself for anyone else, you have to take care of yourself first.

If you're currently a parent or will be soon, remember you're teaching your children how to live. You're a living, breathing example they'll mirror in their own lives. Do you think they deserve better than the way things have been in your own life? If you do, then you need to take this lesson to heart, and realize they'll have lower standards later if you don't raise yours now.

Use this chapter as a way to learn how to embrace everything you are. You're allowed to feel every emotion, and still keep moving forward and living a life of self-love and growth. You're human, and you're allowed to occasionally feel tired and average. The only thing you aren't allowed to do is be content with where you are, and stop challenging yourself to continue learning and growing each and every day.

Selflovology Tips for Balance

- Make a list of what you do and why you do it.

- Based on your list, intentionally choose what you think about and act on. When you put yourself last, you aren't balanced.

- Avoid burnout by being balanced. Every day, allot time for being alone with yourself.

- Stop comparing yourself to others and your perfect version of yourself. Don't let less-than-ness prevent you from loving your-self.

Chapter 13

Today (Not Tomorrow)

> *"The most difficult thing is the decision to act; the rest is merely tenacity... The procedure—the process—is its own reward."*
>
> **Amelia Earhart**

Mastering self-love is about loving the journey. If you're living for a moment in the future (whether it's a graduation, promotion, or new job), you're putting your happiness on hold.

If you try to refocus on today (not tomorrow), you aren't going to prevent that future event from happening. Instead, it will spark your excitement and enjoyment, and make you even more likely to take steps towards your success.

Also, it's important for me to take this moment to remind you that no one is promised tomorrow. Do not put off the things that you can do to better yourself today.

Today is all you have. Live this way. Live like each day is your last. Living in the now will revolutionize how you move throughout your days. The things that you may have once ignored—to be dealt with on another day—will get done.

Living in the here and now will open your eyes to the gravity of your daily decisions and actions. Do not delay living your life in abundance. Do not delay the activities that set your own precious heart afire. Do not delay the good and powerful work you have to offer the world.

Daily Reward

My own today (not tomorrow) moment came when I realized I was setting myself up for disappointment, and wasn't enjoying my life in the moment. Entrepreneurs and other career-minded individuals are frequently focused on their goals, so they forget to live life to the fullest every day.

Instead, they put in passionless hours and wait for the weekend. Or they get distracted and don't achieve their goal because they can't feel the rewards yet.

I'm here to tell you that you can feel rewarded every day. Remember the gold dots? You can break up your goals into smaller chunks, and give yourself a gold dot every day.

This continual striving to do more—create more—is not sustainable. You cannot give from an empty cup. You must build time into your days for deliberate self-care and self-love practices.

Do not fall prey to the tyranny of the urgent. If you take the time to do loving things for yourself your work will become better and more meaningful. Your work will become a clearer and more beautiful reflection of yourself.

This Is Your Time

What are you waiting for? There's a whole community out there ready to cheer you on and lift you up, even if you haven't found them yet. You found this book, which means your self-love needs you to take action today. Then your tomorrow will be beyond your wildest dreams.

The action you take depends on the specifics of your dreams. By gradually balancing the physical, emotional, and financial aspects of your life, you can move forward, despite anything that's holding you back.

If you take simple actions in all of these areas, they will add up to mastering your self-love in a way that fits you. Perhaps you have your physical health figured out, but you lack confidence in the emotional side of things. I also meet people who are emotionally and physically balanced, but still struggle with the financial side of their lives.

Usually, they don't believe me when I tell them their finances are tied to their self-love, but it's true. If you don't have balance in these areas, you will struggle and experience disharmony.

To clarify, today (not tomorrow) also means dealing with unpleasantness right away, rather than putting it off. It means getting started right now, even if things are hard and uncertain.

Here's my message to everyone across this beautiful planet: Life is happening for you right now. The world is waiting for you to discover it. So believe in yourself, and start the process of living the beautiful life you envision.

Your process begins with truly knowing and accepting yourself. This will lead to self-love. It's the foundation for expressing love to everyone you encounter.

A Fresh Start

People talk about love all the time. It's in our music, movies, marketing, and media, so it's on most people's minds.

Too many people come out of the school system loathing their lives and not loving themselves. Society wants every person to fit into a mold they create for them, because it makes them more comfortable.

If anyone is uncomfortable with someone else's label, it's because they don't love themselves. If they haven't found their self-love, they're not looking inward for their light and their purpose.

Today, many people in your life will actively prevent you from taking action. They'll tell you that:

- You are where you live.

- You are your local sports team.

- You are the hot beverage you drink.

- You are a political party.

- You are a race.

- You are a religion.

- You are a generation.

- You are what you wear.

- You are what you listen to.

The world is full of interesting, entertaining distractions. So even with the determination to move forward, you may lose momentum in the work you need to do on yourself. Then your attention gets diverted to outside stimuli telling you where you fit into the world.

Here's the problem: The world wants you to love *it*, not yourself. If you don't love yourself, you'll seek validation from the world—in the form of likes, comments, new clothes, or the latest technology.

Very few people will tell you who you're meant to be. They'll encourage you to be who they want you to be, for whatever reason—likely because they have not done the work towards self-love.

Love is not a switch you turn on or off for each category you correctly choose. We try to seek happiness and love from the people in our lives, but we rarely look within. Some people believe that looking within will only remind them of how messed up they are, how much pain there is, and how far away their destination is.

But in reality, it's the exact opposite. If you look within and face your truth, you will find contentment, peace of mind, true love, joy, and the knowledge that you're beautiful just the way you are. No one will be able to do or say anything to change who you are, or how you feel about yourself.

Remember, anything that anyone says and does has more to do with them than about you. So you can start fresh. For today, face yourself and look within, because an unexamined life isn't a life that's fully lived.

The Dream Within

For a moment, put aside everything external, including the people closest to you, your expectations, and your deadlines. Don't allow anything from the outside world to enter your mind, and focus on loving yourself. Now think about all those outside influences, and prepare to release them.

Take a breath, and exhale everything out of your body and your mind. As you read the next section, don't allow those old emotions and wounds into your mind. Instead, focus on what you're going to achieve.

For now, you have no agenda—nothing to gain or lose.

Now repeat after me:

"Loving myself means being who I am."

It's one thing to repeat this statement, but it's quite another to believe it. However, if you repeat it to yourself every day, you'll start seeing how true it is.

Now let's take it a step further: If you want to live a life of purpose, you have to be who you are. Everything you want to achieve can be yours.

If you can move past seeking empty platitudes and towards the big scary dreams you have for yourself, you'll start changing your frame of mind today (not tomorrow).

It all comes down to taking charge of your life, and choosing the direction you're going to proceed in. So make choices to improve your circumstances, be accountable to yourself, and know that you'll find self-love along the way.

Taking responsibility for what you want in life is a lot more positive and productive than blaming others or expecting handouts.

When you were a little kid, you probably complained to your mom that you were bored. I'm willing to bet that most of your mothers didn't hand over an exciting new game, snack, and adventure every time you whined. It's more likely she suggested you clean your room or do your homework.

Life is like that. If you leave it up to others to fulfill your hopes and dreams, you're likely to find that their suggestion isn't what you'd planned. However, if you depend on yourself and try to find your hopes and dreams within, you'll soon be moving toward them.

Every day, remind yourself that you're responsible for:

- Your own happiness.

- Your self-love and self-worth, and the decisions you make.

- The people you choose to surround yourself with.

- The way you react to situations, both positive and negative.

- The way you feel, think, and act.

- The way you seek out and live your purpose.

Your Ultimate Purpose

Understand that it's okay to walk away from people, places, and things that create toxicity and drama. When you do, your life transformation will begin. Then you'll no longer get caught up in worldly, consumerist, or social expectations. Instead, you focus on self-love, and everything—absolutely everything—will come from within. When you give love, you get love.

All of the pain and failure in your life is growth, and growth always leads to self-love. As your self-love grows, you'll start thanking those that have wronged you. This radical act of forgiveness will become your impetus to take action towards betterness.

If someone tells me about something someone said about me behind my back, I use it as a reason to grow. People have done some downright awful things to me, but I've turned these things into my greatest strengths. Without those people, I wouldn't have become the man I am today.

Once you've learned to love yourself, you understand that hatred isn't about you. The way you react to their self-hatred says everything about you. Know this distinction, and look within; there's no better place to start.

When you find who you are within, you'll uncover your purpose and passion. But first, you must find self-love, because you won't have the confidence to chase your dream until you completely love yourself. Otherwise, you'll let doubt creep in from the many influences that want to tell you who to be and how to act.

Some won't love the fact that you love yourself. Love yourself anyway. Whatever it takes, love yourself anyway. Make your self-mastery happen today. Each time you feel uncertain, know that your self-love isn't something that happens immediately.

Loving yourself is a process, not an end result. Simply put, you have to put the work in every day to move towards your ultimate purpose. Anything else in life isn't fulfillment. You may find a little bit of happiness, but you must renew your fulfillment every single day. And it starts by finding that purpose.

What makes your spirit come alive? Answer this question for yourself and allow the fire within to be a reminder and a roadmap for where you are going in life. If something doesn't light you up from the inside out—that's not your path. You have everything within you to show yourself the way.

Trust yourself. Trust the fire.

Summary of Today

Start today by shifting your focus. When you love yourself, you take a step forward every single day. We've already discussed that pain is a step forward in your life. Pain and adversity are ways to learn about yourself, and reflect on your next decision.

Decide today within yourself that you will:

- Start a small daily habit that will build momentum.

- Focus on turning your passion into a paycheck.

- Practice that hobby you love, but never seem to have time for.

- Reflect on something you're eager to change about yourself.

- Take action on something you've been avoiding for a while.

When you make these choices, you'll find self-love, so you can master everything else you want to accomplish. Pick one thing from the above list, and commit to it for a week, then a month, then a year. And find out what happens when you start today.

Instead of reacting to something that someone said or did, think about the way you're processing the situation. If you choose not to allow others to decide your emotions for you, you'll start looking within.

Eventually, it becomes clear that it's better to be around people that uplift you. Haters will only drain you because that's where they are in their own lives.

Surround yourself with others who are learning and striving to love and accept themselves. These are your people. They will propel you on and lift you up when the road gets tough, and you will do the same for them.

Soon, you will become magnetic. Your love will be like a light to the world drawing in other seekers of love and light. You will create a beautiful community of enlightened souls—I simply can't think of a better way to live life.

Selflovology Tips for Today

- Do something today that your future self will thank you for.

- Stop waiting for the perfect time; the perfect time is now.

- Do one thing to overcome your fear of the future, so it won't prevent your happiness today.

- Feel what's going on around you, and focus on loving yourself and the people in your life who show up today.

- Know that loving yourself is a daily process, so find something to love along every part of the journey.

- Remember that life is happening for you. So shift your focus to the beautiful life you're living.

Chapter 14

Speaking from the Heart

> *"You will know the truth, and the truth will set you free."*
>
> **John 8:32 NIV**

Speaking from the heart sounds easy enough, doesn't it? So why do so many of us spend our whole lives saying everything except what our hearts are telling us? Here's the simple answer: That's what we've been trained to do, ever since we were little.

At some point too long ago to remember, people classified your vulnerability as being weak and uncomfortable, and therefore unsuitable for discussion. So you were taught to internalize and marginalize everything your heart was saying in order to keep conversations light and pleasant. Why should you make anyone else aware of the daily struggles and internal battles we all face? Sounds silly, doesn't it?

Suffering in Silence

We all go through the same things. We all feel doubt, guilt, shame, worry, and embarrassment. We all wonder if we're doing the right thing. We all tell each other well-rehearsed stories about how our lives should look, then cringe when we fail to live up to these standards. We all go through it, but we've learned not to speak about it.

Where does this silence leave us? Just look at the world we live in. How many people feel alone because they aren't speaking from their hearts? And how many of us feel overwhelmed by the world telling us that speaking our truth makes everyone around us uncomfortable?

I would argue that a majority of people feel very alone with their feelings. They may be surrounded by friends and family—sharing surface level conversations—but few are sharing the deep feelings of their hearts. I think this is the truest definition of loneliness.

When you cannot sit across a table from someone and look them straight in the eyes and say what you are feeling deep within, you will never feel truly seen or heard.

It's very sad, really. We are all walking around in silence for no reason. We all share these deep feelings, and we all share the need to connect with others on a very deep level, yet we aren't doing so.

The programming of our past and the unspoken and spoken rules about sharing our feelings is insidious. We've been told for far too long that our feelings don't matter. We don't feel worthy of a compassionate witness to our inner lives.

You've been programmed to both suffer and thrive in silence, so you won't sound like a downer or a braggart. After all, who likes those kinds of people? Subsequently, you've dulled your ability to connect with the side of yourself that allows you to speak your truth. You may be reading this and thinking, "Now what?"

Perhaps you've lost touch with yourself to the point that you have a hard time tapping into your heart's language. And you've learned that speaking from the heart is frowned upon by society. So what can you do?

Let Go of Fear

Learn to listen to yourself more, and speak from a place of abundance and vulnerability, rather than a place of shame and doubt. And give others the space to do the same.

To help you connect with your heart, let everything go that stops you from speaking your truth. For most people, this silence is due to an overwhelming fear of:

- What people will think.

- What people will say about us when we're not around.

- What speaking your mind might do to the people around you.

- Who may be forced out of your life, especially people you don't want to let go of.

Trust me, I hear you. Fear is one of the most motivational and destructive emotions. It can make you accept things you never thought you would. It can keep you in a place, even though you know it's not where you'll be happiest. It cements your feet to the ground, when all you long to do is fly.

But fear comes from maintaining your facade. The faster you can get rid of the facade you've been building all your life, the faster you'll come back to a place where you can access your true, unprotected heart.

Finding Workarounds

For a moment, ask yourself, "What's keeping me from speaking my heart?" If fear is involved in any of the reasons you come up with, it means you're out of alignment. If you're aligned with yourself, there's no room for fear.

If you're following your gut and your heart, there's no reason to be afraid, because you know deep-down why you're doing what you're doing. If you're able to convince yourself otherwise, your walls are still up. Stop making excuses about why you can't speak your mind, and stop living in fear. Then you can start giving yourself permission to access your heart.

Believe it or not, the walls you've built up not only keep others out, but also make it harder for you to see yourself for who you really are.

Slowly begin to tear down these walls to reveal all that you are inside and out. When you begin sharing you will feel the weight of all that you have been carrying become lighter and lighter. You were never meant to carry all of your feelings alone. We are relational people who need others to bear witness to our inner lives and we need to be that person for others as well.

Happy Baby

I want you to do this exercise with me. Close your eyes. Imagine yourself as a baby. You are defenseless, and have no concern for anything but yourself. You're vulnerable because you don't how to take care of yourself yet. Take yourself back to that place.

Allow yourself to shed all those years of learning, erase all the pain you've endured, and unravel all the protections you've built around you. Feel how at peace you are when you just exist. You're not here to do anything other than just exist. You haven't learned what to say (and not to say), what to feel, and how to react. And you haven't endured pain, suffering, trauma, love, and heartbreak. You're just you.

In that moment, feel how light your soul is. Now open your eyes, and take ownership of all the weight you've added to your life since you were born. What weight are you carrying around that's protecting you from threats that are no longer in your presence?

How many scars are you still tending to, even though they healed years ago? You don't have to be afraid of being yourself. Your thoughts and words have a place in this world. So own them, embrace them, and connect with your heart.

When you do so, you will find your people—the people who are safe and offer a soft place to land, to share, and to connect on the deepest levels.

Stuck on Repeat

Stop telling yourself the same sorry excuses for why you can't be open and honest. When you keep recounting the same reasons why you can't be honest with yourself, you sound like a broken record.

Clearly, there are already enough people out there repeating other people's stories and beliefs. You don't need to be another one of them. Realize that your truth is better than any other version of reality that you could speak.

Your truth matters. It's important. It's worthy to be spoken and shared. Sometimes you have to just trust, open your mouth, and the words will find their way from your heart to the hearts of those around you.

Speaking with Confidence

People are drawn to people who speak their truth with confidence. You don't have to minimize your success or lie about your pain points to make others comfortable. Instead, be comfortable with your true self, and speak your truth with confidence. Step into your power, and own that your truth is good enough.

Practice slowing yourself down while you're having a conversation. Speak with purpose and intention, rather than just filling the silence. Our words create the space we occupy, so make sure you're conscious about your word choices and the way you speak.

What it really boils down to is confidence. You have to believe that your thoughts are worth something. And more than that, you must have the confidence to practice speaking your truth, regardless of the outcome.

I'm not telling you to shout at every person who cuts you off on the freeway, or to be rude to the lady in your office that always asks the same questions. However, I am telling you to stop being afraid of your truth. Know that speaking from the heart will never lead you astray. Speaking your own truth—and not someone else's—is the only way to live life on your own terms.

Summary of Speaking

Here's one thing that I frequently encounter in people: They don't speak their truth, but they somehow expect the people around them to know how they feel. In addition to this unattainable expectation, these people usually never get what they actually desire, because they don't offer the world their true, heartfelt opinions.

In order to get the most out of life, you must be willing to honestly interact with the world, which includes speaking your truth. If you never tell the world what you want, you'll never get what you desire.

Speaking from your heart is the most sincere and authentic way to find self-love. No one can read your mind, so unless you ask the world for what you want, you'll never receive it.

Learn to embrace yourself, your thoughts, and your feelings. Learn to speak from a place of truth, and don't restrain your authentic self for some silly reason that doesn't make sense. Free yourself, and see how your life changes.

Selflovology Tips for Speaking

- Always and only speak the truth.

- Learn how to be open about how you feel. Have confidence in yourself enough to speak up.

- Let go of the stories you tell yourself that hold you back. Allow yourself to overcome negative thoughts from the past. Feel at peace with who you are: both good and bad.

- Visualize how you want to sound, and practice slowing down.

- Learn to listen to yourself.

Chapter 15

Life Transformation

"Once you become very aware of yourself, it's almost a joke when someone tries to tell you about it."

Jet Li

Part of mastering self-love is understanding that the journey is never really over. There's always more to learn. But the unique part about the journey of mastering self-love is that you learn to appreciate and understand each and every part of your self-discovery. So it becomes less about the destination, and more about each step that you take.

We all make choices to be more aware, strive for better, and focus on the present, and these choices help us master our hearts and thoughts as we keep seeking betterness in our lives.

The Beauty in the Journey

The purpose of this chapter is to remind you about the immense beauty in the journey to self-understanding. If you've gotten this far in this book, I know you're serious about finding yourself, so you already know that falling in love with yourself will allow you to fully embrace your life, love, and experiences.

I want to take a minute and remind you that this journey takes a lot of courage. And as we've seen, it isn't always pretty, and it won't always make sense to you or the people you're closest to. But in this moment, I want to acknowledge you and tell you—from my heart to yours—that I'm proud of everything you are and everything you're becoming.

Now let's return our attention to this whirlwind of a journey called *Selflovology*.

Overcoming Misconceptions

Let's start by taking a minute to think about how long it took to build up the misconceptions you have about yourself. It took years of your teachers, parents, family members, and friends telling you what you can and cannot do. Regardless of their intentions, every single person in your life has impacted your perception of yourself.

Do you wonder why so many people in this world feel lost? We're constantly bombarded by other people's perceptions of us. Here's the silly thing: These perceptions are created without anyone actually knowing what's going on in our minds. But we use these perceptions to define ourselves anyway. So now can you understand why learning to master self-love often requires a lot of unlearning?

The purpose of life transformation is to inspire yourself, so you can get out of your own way. It's time to move forward with your own special purpose. However, once you understand that your self-love is your very own (and no one else's), you'll set yourself free.

Through self-love, you have an extraordinary understanding of what brings you joy and fulfills you. Therefore, you'll be able to move forward with your life, without questioning your motives and actions. Instead, you'll learn how to filter people, places, and things that are threatening your hard-earned sense of peace. A lot of people are still struggling to understand this concept: Something may be the right thing for you to do, even if everyone doesn't understand why you're doing it.

We all have room to learn. I'm not suggesting you become self-righteous, and live your life with the idea that you can do no wrong; that's certainly not what self-love is all about. Instead, it's about coming to peace with yourself and creating the self-awareness that you're able to filter out everything that used to hold you back in your life.

Falling in love with yourself involves:

- Breaking down all the walls around yourself.
- Allowing yourself to feel what it means to truly and authentically be yourself.
- Finding it inside of yourself to let that be enough.

It's not about others understanding and accepting you. It's about understanding and accepting yourself, so you'll be secure in yourself, despite anything that happens.

You Are Who You Are

When you're your authentic self, you exude positivity, because you're living from a place of honesty that reveals your true self. Now isn't the time to be hesitant—life is too short to waste any more time—so go after it with everything you've got.

If you follow someone else's dream for your life, it's very unlikely that you'll be successful. And if you try to do that, it will probably bring nothing but misery and despair. So, what's the secret to freedom and happiness? Here's one good place to start: Having no expectations of others, and not allowing other people's expectations to affect the direction of your life transformation.

If you live under the weight of expectations, you live in fear. You'll always desire a certain outcome, which may or may not happen.

Whether you know it or not, you're definitively attached to an outcome: You hope something will happen, and you hope something else will not happen. When you're free of expectations, you can go with the flow of life, and you won't be as affected by the outcome. Instead, you'll know that every outcome—whether good or bad—can serve to move you toward a greater understanding of your identity and your desires.

If you release your expectations, you'll allow yourself to experience freedom and happiness. Like everything on the journey to self-love, this experience won't occur overnight; it requires an understanding about the ways your expectations are holding you back. Remember, you have one chance to live your life, so don't waste another second worrying about disappointing anyone. The people who really care about you will be with you, no matter what you do and who you become.

This is not a dress rehearsal. This is your one wild and crazy chance at living the life you desire. Do not delay. You will never regret time spent learning more about yourself, accepting all that you have been, and look forward with grace and gratitude to all that you will become.

I really cannot think of anything more exciting. I get butterflies in my stomach just thinking of the freedom and possibilities that will come into your life when you make the decision to really do the work of self-love.

The Internal Mirror

We spend most of our lives worrying about perfection. How do we look to others? We get so busy looking in the mirror to change how we look on the outside that we don't try to cover up what's on the inside.

We may believe that if we're not perfect, no one will see us, find us beautiful, or possibly even love us. But by mastering self-love, we can move away from this harmful habit, and stop relying on the mirror to tell us what we are.

Here's what you may not realize: The mirror was never meant to be your enemy. Rather, it was meant to let you see all of your beauty.

Even though the mirror never changed, the person I saw in it did. While I was finding my self-love, it took a long time to realize that my self-talk was making me hate the person I saw in the mirror. I was at war with myself.

Now take a moment to look in the mirror. Take a deep breath and really look deep into your own eyes. Notice that you can see a little sparkle of your soul. There is pure magic within you just waiting to emerge. Allowing this magic to fully bloom is the work of your life. It's exciting, and scary, and wonderful all at the same time. Discover how beautiful you are as a creation.

What can you see, smell, taste, feel, and hear? Spend a moment feeling your lungs feeding your body oxygen, and your muscles holding you upright.

You are amazing, so there's no need to fight with yourself. Let yourself become the lover of your own soul, your best friend, and your closest confidant. Once you can see yourself underneath the wall of wounds you've built up, it's time to come to peace with your demons, your pain, and your adversity. Then and only then, you can start getting to the place of accepting and loving yourself.

When you're ready, repeat after me. "Self-love is more important to me than:

- Needing validation that what I'm doing is worthy.

- Needing a person, place, or thing to fill me with a sense of purpose.

- Needing to impress others or fit in.

- Needing to be part of something."

Remember, the mirror never changes. The person we see in it can change as soon as we open our hearts to self-love.

World Transformation

By living your truth and getting to know yourself, the trial and error you experience along the journey to self-love will become a stepping stone to a life well-lived. When you're being true to yourself (not living to impress people or receive validation), your life truly transforms.

If you follow this trajectory, your life transformation will turn into a world transformation. Self-love removes hatred from the equation. Once you love yourself and are committed to transforming your life into one of opportunity, you're no longer competing with anyone. You're the only person you have to compare yourself to.

By falling in love with yourself, you see the world through a new lens, and approach people with an optimistic, open heart. Working on self-love leaves no room for fear-based reactions, so instead, you lift others up alongside you. In a way, falling in love with yourself is also falling in love with your surroundings and situations.

The Cure to Self-Hatred

How can this message of self-love reach more people and become the cure to self-hatred? How can it reach those who need it most (such as people who are contemplating suicide)? By choosing self-love, you're a living example, so you're preventing somebody else from giving up. Remind yourself that all the adversity you face will turn you into a better version of yourself.

Life transformation is a truly powerful concept. In fact, it's somewhat intimidating, right? You might be wondering what life transformation has to do with self-love.

Falling in love with yourself requires fearless courage, so you need to acquire a strong, unshakable sense of self. Then no matter what happens, you'll choose not to quit while you're on your journey to self-love. Oftentimes, loving yourself requires huge changes. Why? Because many of us have built an entire life without self-love.

The House of Self-Love

Therefore, without self-awareness, choosing a path to self-love means that foundational shifts in your life will have to occur.

Consider this analogy: You buy a beautiful house that serves its purpose. The roof doesn't leak, and your heater and AC work well. But unfortunately, you don't perform the routine maintenance on your house that will keep it functioning at its highest potential.

Then one winter, a branch from a tree in your backyard snaps, and strikes your house. It causes a couple of the roof tiles to crack. So every time it rains, the wood and insulation underneath the tiles are exposed to water. Then as time goes by, they start rotting.

It takes time, but you eventually save up enough money to fix the roof. It's sustained heavy water damage, and the whole thing needs to be replaced. To add insult to injury, the repairperson tells you that it wouldn't have cost much if you'd gotten it repaired when it happened. You kick yourself for letting it get to the point that the entire insulation and wood beams have to be replaced. In addition, there are water spots on the ceiling underlying the damaged area.

Now you have to hire a painter to repair the ugly spots that make you cringe when you have company over. But little by little, you fix it, so you start hoping that the house can be saved with the right tender love and care.

You've worked so hard that you decide to redecorate. You go and buy new carpets for the living room. You get new wallpaper for the kitchen, and even splurge and buy yourself a beautiful new bathtub.

You feel elated. It's very similar to the way you feel after you transform your life. It's a long, painstaking process. It takes time, work, and persistence. It requires you to dig up your past, tend to your unhealed wounds, and find peace. You need to be willing to fix the holes in your roof and replace the old emotional wounds that fester with pain and anger.

Life transformation is the process of finding self-love. Throughout this process, you're fixing, noticing, learning, and healing. The journey of self-love means transforming your thinking, your feelings, and your understanding of yourself and your life. Not everyone will like your new house, but that doesn't matter because you love it. You feel proud and passionate about what you've created.

Summary of Transformation

The journey is not in the result, but everything you learned along the way. Running from your problems or covering them with false pride, insecurities, overcompensated ego, or anything else won't heal anything or anyone. Choosing self-love has allowed you to transform your life into something you can be proud of.

Finding self-love means you have to be willing to let go of everything you've learned over the course of your entire life. You have to be okay with the fact that some people will never understand your process. And sadly, some of those people may be the ones closest to you. But you know the beautiful thing about finding your self-love. It won't matter to you anymore, because you know what you did was the right thing for you to do. No one has to understand that, other than you.

Truth be told, some people won't like what you've chosen to do. Some people are happy staying in the same place throughout their lives, so they may see this new change in you as silly, radical, or outright stupid. And that's okay; that's where they are in their lives.

You have to feel comfortable in your own skin, to the point that nothing that anyone else says can steal your peace of mind. As long as you're following your heart, you're on the right path. And the things that show up in your life to deter you from your ultimate peace of mind, may need to be replaced with things that support you along this journey. Remember, your happiness is your own; it cannot be felt or defined by anyone else.

Selflovology Tips for Transformation

- Make a commitment to yourself to build a better you.

- Find a motivational partner.

- Carve out time for your physical, mental, emotional, and spiritual lives. Turn off the electronic distractions, and tune into your self-love.

- Stop preventing life from happening to you. As an exercise, spend a few hours mentally allowing your passion to take you in any direction it takes you in, even if it seems crazy or impossible.

- Life transformation happens due to self-love. Don't wait for your life to transform; live it now.

Chapter 16

Choosing a Beautiful Life

> *"The most liberating thing about beauty is realizing that you are the beholder. This empowers us to find beauty in places where others have not dared to look, including inside ourselves."*
>
> **Salma Hayek**

After 24 years, I came to this realization: Beauty comes from within, so anything you're looking for must be cultivated in yourself first. And when I say anything—I mean anything. If you will simply master yourself, you can have any beautiful life you imagine.

Here are some cause-effect relationships related to having a beautiful life:

- To see beauty in the world, you must master your inner beauty.

- To view life as a beautiful gift, you must give yourself the gift of self-love.

- To find happiness in relationships, you must master inner happiness.

- To achieve wealth and abundance, you must appreciate your abundant number of God-given talents.

- To have a healthy body, you must have a healthy mind.

- To have success in life, you must successfully master your own inner challenges.

- To know the world, you must know yourself.

- To be loved, you must love yourself.

Choosing Self-Love

No one forces you to enter any relationship, and this realization is an important part of the journey to self-love. We choose others, and based on that choice, we allow people to treat us the way we really feel about ourselves. As adults, our self-abuse (or lack of self-love) often prefaces the physical, verbal, and mental abuse others inflict on us.

When we don't know our identity or our worth, we open the doors to anyone and everyone, and end up tolerating and accepting toxic behaviors. And if you accept these unhealthy behaviors, it says a lot about where you are inside. If you truly love yourself, you'll have the strength to put an end to the unhealthy relationships in your life.

Life is a test. You can't control many things, but you can make these choices:

- Masking your pain, or facing it.

- Hurting those who hurt you, or loving them from afar.

- Believing that this moment is the beginning of something, or the end of something.

- Focusing on yourself, or entirely forgetting about yourself.

You must choose to practice love. Loving yourself is not selfish; it's necessary. Even if you care deeply about somebody, you won't be able to sustain a relationship with that person unless you love yourself first.

Choose yourself every day. Be there for yourself every day. Make the positive difference you want to see in this life, and you can be there for others in ways you never thought possible.

You will become more wholehearted and every decision or relationship will take on deeper meaning. You will show up as the full expression of yourself.

Imagine if we all did this—pursued self-love and wholehearted living. Imagine if all our relationships and experiences were rich and beautifully fulfilling. It would life-changing... world-changing in fact.

Being Accountable for Self-Love

Every day, count yourself in, and make time for your first love: self-love. You are worth it, and you are amazing. We have all been given such a beautiful life, which we can use to learn and grow together.

Tell those around you that you're choosing betterness, not bitterness. Then move on towards positivity.

Wherever you are as you're reading this book, know this: It's not too late. Returning to the gold dots, find someone to share your gold dot moment with right now. Choose someone you love; it could be your friend, partner, or family member.

Now take time to fully articulate your gold dot moment. Look ten years into the future, and in detail, imagine the life you've created for yourself. Then take those stickers, and put them everywhere. Use them as reminders about where you're going, and use your subconscious mind to be the pathway that will get you there.

Summary of Beautiful Life

When you work toward your purpose, fear is eliminated. When you do what you were meant to do, your self-love will bloom. So work on yourself, and don't be afraid to face your reality.

When you choose to look in the mirror and accept everything you are, you can move forward from a place of joy. Choose to love yourself throughout your entire life, not just in the easy moments. Remember, you can choose to love yourself and be filled with a joy that surpasses everything.

Ask yourself, "What am I afraid of?" There's a difference between being nervous and having fear. If you know what you're here for (and doing what you know is right), nervousness will be common, but fear won't. Don't fear your purpose. Find your element, and stay in it. Take that risk because you know it's what sets your soul on fire.

When you truly know and love yourself, you will live a beautiful life.

Selflovology Tips for a Beautiful Life

- Take time to appreciate the life you've been given. You are beautiful, and you're here to share that beauty. Beauty always comes from within. We choose how we see the world, so we can choose to see it as beautiful.

- Assess your relationships. They reflect the way you feel about yourself.

- Pinpoint the pursuit that will make your heart soar. When you work on your passion, fear is eliminated.

- To live your life on your terms, start by figuring out what's stopping you.

Conclusion

Master Yourself, Master Your Universe

"Knowing others is intelligence; knowing yourself is true wisdom. Mastering others is strength; mastering yourself is true power."

Lao Tzu

When you arrive at the end of your journey to self-love, you realize that it was ultimately leading you to find long-lasting peace and happiness, even though it's not always pretty or perfect.

Maybe you chose to read this book because you felt like you didn't have direction and needed guidance. Or maybe you read it because you're going through a life shift, and felt like more fully understanding self-love would help you make sense of all the chaos. Or maybe you just felt like it was time to delve deeper into the definition of truly loving yourself.

A Moment of Introspection

Whatever the reason, I want you to take a moment now to reflect on what you've read, and think about which parts spoke to you most during your journey to self-love. Why am I asking you to perform this introspection? Because the self-love journey means something different to everyone.

We each have our strengths and weaknesses within our journey toward self-love. This journey is less about reinventing the wheel, and more about learning our weaknesses and pain points, and allowing ourselves to heal those pieces.

We are not perfect, nor will we ever be. But that's not the point of self-love anyway. The true goal is to find out who you are, and to learn to accept and love your entire self. Life is challenging enough without fighting yourself day in and day out.

Throughout my personal journey, I've repeatedly learned this lesson: If I allow myself to be my own best friend, my journey never feels lonely or overwhelming.

In this conclusion to *Selflovology*, I want to revisit some major themes by briefly exploring five lessons about maintaining and growing your self-love every day. Use them as reminders of what you've accomplished by taking the time to invest in yourself.

Lesson 1: Self-love Is Your Responsibility

Don't be daunted by this lesson. The fact that you're in control of your own happiness is a beautiful thing.

Sometimes, we make other people's responsibilities and happiness our burdens, and allow ourselves to carry these responsibilities for others. Why? Because we love the people closest to us. But the most freeing part of finding our own self-love is realizing that we're only responsible for ourselves.

We don't need to be weighed down by the other responsibilities or burdens we place on ourselves. We're not responsible for anything other than our own happiness and peace of mind. Now this lesson doesn't sound daunting, does it? The most freeing feeling in the world is letting other people choose their life paths, and decide what they want to do and feel. And we can do the same for ourselves.

Ultimately, being in love with yourself allows you to escape from the mental fog of taking on more than you have to, and coming to the realization that you're only in control of yourself. It's not your responsibility to fix everyone else's problems, struggles, and emotional sludge. These burdens aren't ours to carry or drown in. However, that doesn't mean that we can't empathize with and help others throughout our daily lives. But remember, there's a big difference between supporting someone and making another person's problems your own.

Lesson 2: Some Walls Were Built to Be Torn Down

We're not meant to live in boxes. Your mind shouldn't be limited by preconceived notions about what you can and can't be, or what you should or shouldn't do. Just as a flower will never grow if its roots are constricted by a tiny pot, you'll never grow into your fullest potential if you limit your room to grow.

All the limiting things you tell yourself have to stop. You're not helping yourself by telling yourself no. In fact, you're stealing your chance to have boundless growth and joy—by letting your insecurities, your scarcity mindset, your self-criticism, and your fear win. When you find self-love, you'll eliminate a tremendous amount of fear and insecurity.

If you try something new and fail, who cares? Were you able to ride a bike perfectly the first time your parents took the training wheels off? Of course not. But did that stop you from trying again? If someone is expecting you to be perfect in every way, tell them that their expectations are unreasonable.

Stop expecting perfection from yourself. You are good enough. It's not embarrassing that you aren't a savant at everything you do. You might be chuckling right now, because it sounds funny.

But the truth is that many of us limit ourselves because:

- We're afraid of failing.

- We're afraid of looking dumb.

- Most of all, we're afraid that failing will make others think less of us.

But many people don't realize that you're winning *because* you're trying. You've overcome the box that many of us are afraid to even touch. You might feel like you're failing, but if you keep trying, you'll get better with each attempt. Set yourself free, and stop worrying so much about the outcome. Love yourself enough to give yourself the opportunity to grow. Don't let fear or embarrassment stand in your way.

Lesson 3: You Are Amazing

I can't tell you how many people I've heard talking about how great, intelligent, or appealing other people are, while failing to acknowledge their own brilliance. Give yourself the credit you deserve. It's easy for us to look at others and only see a fraction of what's actually going on with them. We think, "Wow, that person has life figured out." Or, "Wow, all I want is for my life to be that perfect." Here's what people fail to realize: Each of us knows ourselves a lot better than anyone else possibly could.

Even if we tried, we couldn't share everything we think about, even over the course of a single day. We're at home with our thoughts, so it is easy to look around and think, "Wow I am so much less amazing than that person." But that's not the case. Just because you can't see or hear other people's thoughts, that doesn't mean they don't have less going on in their minds. Ultimately, if we were able to be as intimately connected with another person as we are with ourselves, we would soon realize we're all the same.

Don't let someone else's outward presentation make you question your intrinsic worth. That's not self-love. Along your journey to self-love, you'll find that you can admire others, empathize with others, support others, laugh with others, and even cry with others. But that shouldn't affect how you feel about yourself. By finding true self-love, you find true self-acceptance and understand your self-worth, beyond the boundaries of comparisons.

Every day, make it a habit to remind yourself how amazing you are. You are on this earth for a reason, and you're doing your best. You've never left your side or given up on yourself. You're here, and that's amazing.

Lesson 4: The Root of Self-Love Is Self-Acceptance

No amount of self-improvement can ever make up for a lack of self-acceptance. You have to accept all of yourself, not just the pretty parts and happy times.

It's so easy to:

- Be self-conscious about all of our so-called flaws.

- Listen to the people around us.

- Let other's opinions create our feeling of worthiness.

- Feel like you're not good enough, or that your life isn't as perfect as someone else's.

All of those things are easy. But do they serve you in any way? No.

In order to find self-love, you have to learn that you should celebrate everything you are. You may hate certain tendencies, or you may feel you're a little broken or jaded from past experiences. But let me tell you, none of those things define you more than what you choose to do for yourself each day.

You can choose to love yourself. You can decide to celebrate each and every part of yourself, just as you are. Ultimately, the lens you choose to view yourself with is your choice.

You can choose to chide yourself and nitpick the nuances that make you who you are. Or you can step into your power, and know that you're a soul full of love and that you're growing every day. You'll never be perfect, so stop trying to be. But if you choose to accept your imperfections, you'll always be enough. Self-improvement will only lead to deeper self-love if you tune into yourself, fill your soul with fulfillment, and extend kindness to yourself every day.

If you simply go through the motions of self-improvement (such as reading books, going to workshops, and listening to podcasts), you'll never actually improve, and you'll never make it to your destination.

But you can choose to realize you're so special and amazing that you owe yourself the chance to be happier and more aware. Then you'll find self-love, and your self-improvement will naturally occur. And best of all, you'll give yourself the permission to step into your full potential.

Lesson 5: Trust Yourself, Your Thoughts, and Your Journey

On this journey to self-love, nothing is more important than trusting yourself. The older I get, the more I listen to my mind and body when they tell me what's best for me. Why? Because I've come to understand that I have my own best interests at heart, more than anyone else in the world. Likewise, I understand myself more than anyone else.

I'm sure you've heard that all people have opinions. In fact, most people feel that their opinion is superior to others, that they know best, and that their opinions should be accepted and held as the ultimate truth. And if you have this feeling, it's accurate. Your opinions and thoughts are for you. They align with your belief system, and they serve you. But they're only for you.

Ultimately, no matter what others might tell you, it's always imperative that you come back to yourself, and listen to what you're thinking and feeling. You should listen to your intuition, not ignore it.

I've frequently found that people are quick to listen to other's opinions about making decisions when they lack self-love. And while there's nothing wrong with seeking advice from the people around you, there's clearly a problem with allowing others to guide you onto the same life path they're on, and accept their thoughts and feelings as your own.

You're walking your own path—don't ever let someone choose your path for you. Rather than looking to people you trust for advice, check in with yourself first. What do *you* want? What works for *you*? What decision are you fearful of making? Before you invite others to give advice, find clarity within yourself. You know and understand yourself, and your thoughts are there for a reason. Listen to yourself, trust yourself, and give yourself a chance to follow your intuition. You already know the answers. Don't be afraid to acknowledge your truth.

Step away from fear, and take solace in knowing that listening to your heart and mind will never lead you astray. If all your decisions come from your heart and your mind, you'll never live with regret. Everything doesn't always work out perfectly. But when you make your own decisions, they will easily settle in your soul, and align with who you truly are. This is your journey, your story, your life. You get to choose where it takes you. You get to put yourself first. So trust yourself, and know that all experiences in your life serve a purpose.

If you're aligned with yourself, you'll always rest easy at night. Don't be afraid of your power to decide. It's not wrong or selfish to choose yourself first.

Welcome to Self-Love

Ultimately, what is self-love? It's a beautiful and powerful expression of self-acceptance, self-awareness, and self-discipline. It's finding yourself underneath everything you've been taught, and everything you've told yourself for years.

Finding self-love requires the capacity to unlearn things you've believed to be true for many years, and the courage to realize this new path is the right one for you—no matter what anyone else says or does. Finding self-love includes intrinsically finding self-acceptance, and realizing you're only responsible for yourself in this life.

Your only job on this earth is to feed your happiness, and fuel the things that matter to you and bring you good energy. Self-love involves allowing yourself to discern which people, places, and things drain your energy, then allowing them to fall out of your life. Self-love is giving yourself permission to be yourself in a raw, honest, vulnerable way; it's never being ashamed of who you are and aren't.

Falling in love with yourself is very similar to falling in love with another person. First, you see your external self—the shiny version of yourself that you present to the world. Next, you get to know yourself. How do you like your coffee in the morning? How do other people make you feel? What makes you happy? What fills your heart? And as you get to know yourself better, you start to fall in love with all of you—even your quirks. You love the way you don't like sleeping with your feet uncovered, and the way you feel when you hear certain songs.

Here's the most beautiful part: The better you get to know yourself, the more you trust yourself and love your scars.

When you find self-love, you'll fall in love with all that you are and everything you feel and think—because they're expressions of every piece of yourself. Envision the person you love the most. Do you love them for everything they are, even the things they do that drive you crazy, and that you don't understand? Yes, of course you do.

Self-love is a deep, unconditional love for everything you are. It in-cludes the self-awareness to differentiate who you are (and how you feel about yourself) when you're confronted by people and situations that disagree with the self-awareness you've found.

You are a deeply feeling and powerful human being. You are a special, unique miracle. You have purpose, passion, and everything else you need inside of you. You don't need to pretend to be anyone else anymore, or try to impress anyone. You don't need to do anything other than allow yourself to be seen. You are—always have been and always will be—enough, and you're worthy of your own love.

Remember, self-love is the cure to self-hatred, the beginning of self-healing, and the end to self-destruction. So you should whole-heartedly give yourself to your own self-love. Although this road may not always be easy, it will be worth it when you reach your destination. Just keep moving forward. One foot in front of the other. Every single day.

Share with Me

Tell me how you're falling in love with yourself, and let me know if you're struggling with one of the steps. You can engage with others on the self-love journey following @MrSelfLove and @Selflovology on Instagram, and you can check out SelflovologyU.com for more resources.

Also, don't forget to check the *Sel lovology* Tips at the end of each chapter in this book. They're simple, straight-to-the-point remind-ers.

About the Author

Armon Anderson was born and raised in Arizona. He has been a basketball player, professional network marketer, writer, speaker, and self-love coach. He speaks fluent Farsi, is ambidextrous and at one point forgot how to speak English. He now resides in sunny Southern California with his dog Coco.

His debut book *Selflovology* is a self-help book with a great deal of personality. Written in first person, Armon shares his most intimate and formative experiences that led him to finding his own self-love; and inspires readers to look within and find their own self-love through his use of narrative stories, questions and self-love check lists included at the end of each chapter. Together with Armon you will engage in a journey that is sure to make you laugh and cry as you discover your own self-love.